Praise f

MW00946820

"Will show you how improv is done when it's done brilliantly."
— *The Austin Chronicle*

"They have built their own language of improv."
— *The Austin American-Statesman*

"Chris and Tami have made their theaters into welcoming communities for comedians. In a business full of shady clubs and crabby audiences, performing at The New Movement is like going on vacation."

— Eliza Skinner (comedian, *Comedy Central*)

"Chris and Tami are an amazing force - individually as artistic dynamos, and together as an even more powerful dynamo. The sheer volume of art and joy that they have added to the creative scenes in Austin and New Orleans is truly spectacular. What I find particularly inspiring about what they've added is the creation of a community of empowerment. Using the life-changing idea of improvisational theater, combined with their own *joie de vivre*, these two have birthed an environment where others feel safe to take creative risks in order to grow and evolve as human beings. Chris and Tami literally are making the world a better place. So the least you could do is read their book."

— Micah Philbrook (co-founder, pH Comedy Theatre)

"Chris and Tami's passion and commitment to spreading the word about this amazing art form is unparalleled. If you don't read this book, it's because you don't have the fucking guts to do it."

— Brian O'Connell (comedian)

Improv Wins
An Improv Comedy Textbook

BY CHRIS TREW & TAMI NELSON

ILLUSTRATED BY TRUSTON AILLET
EDITED BY BROCK LABORDE

Another great book from Studio8.net!

Improv Wins: An Improv Comedy Textbook

ISBN: 978-1-304-22508-5

Cover design by Henry Linser

Printed in the United States of America

We dedicate this book to all of our past, present and future students.

TABLE OF CONTENTS

How to Approach This Book:
An Introduction

The art of improv is a vague, amoebic thing rich in contradictions.

We love improv.

We love it because of its contradictions and debatable disparities. We love that it's a puzzle that everyone puts together in different ways to make the picture that they think looks best.

In this book, we piece together the puzzle that improv has presented us and show you how we like our pictures to look.

Our approach might not be for everyone, and as with all improv instruction, this is only our opinion.

Use what you like, don't stress about what you don't. We are totally comfortable with you ripping out these pages or deleting them from your hard drive or humming loudly when it comes up in your headphones.

We've logged thousands of hours studying, watching, performing, and teaching improv. What we offer in this book is what we teach in our classes - our personal observations, our opinions, and the perspective we have gained in that time.

We love that improv exists *because* it is an evolving and prismatic thing. That's part of what makes it so exciting to engage in for hours and hours. It's always new, it has no real ending, it regenerates, and it has the ability to surprise and move even the most experienced improviser/audience.

We understand that improv is a very modern art form, that it's still being defined in live theater, and that it has yet to be consumed by popular culture.

We think that's badass.

This book was written by Tami Nelson and Chris Trew.

In the spirit of Improv, we have invited a number of our friends (who happen to be geniuses) to share their ideas and puzzle pieces here, too.

We talked to each other about this book a lot, we've written and erased and rewritten thousands of words, and we stayed up late thinking about what we're trying to say.

We hope you take something fun from this book.

Who We Be:
About the Authors

Hello.

We are Tami Nelson and Chris Trew.

We are BFF's and are writing this book about one of our favorite things in the world.

How I (Tami Nelson) Got Into Improv

So I guess it's like this.

I took a gig dancing go-go in New Orleans sometime in my mid-20's. In retrospect, I understand that I was responding to a need to be onstage, to get in front of an audience to confront myself in the me-mirror or figure out who I really was or some business.

I did a small tour through Louisiana, Mississippi, and Tennessee and learned all I needed to know about go-go dancing: as hard as I tried, it just wasn't funny.

Don't get me wrong - I was a hilarious dancer. But the audience wasn't there to watch fringy mini dress-wearing gals crack silly expressions on the podium; they wanted to boogie. I left the go-go group when I discovered a small improv theater that taught classes in uptown New Orleans.

I saw some shows and thought, "This is terrifying," and immediately enrolled in classes. I painted my teacher's apartment to pay for my classes and quickly became consumed with the art form.

That was 2003.

Soon after I started taking classes, I met Chris Trew. We had an onstage chemistry that thrilled us both, it blossomed into a friendship, and soon we were daydreaming about all the things we could do in this great big comedy world together.

How I (Chris Trew) Got Into Improv

Here's what happened with me.

I wanted to be an actor when I saw *Ace Ventura: Pet Detective*, but then I wanted to do sketch comedy when I saw MTV's *The State*. Then I wanted to do whatever I wanted to when I saw *Sifl and Olly* (also on MTV).

Near the end of my senior year of high school (1999), the internet was becoming "a thing." One of my best friends and I created a humor website that got us into a lot of trouble at school. Even though the expulsion was eventually reduced to a suspension, the seed was planted.

The day after I graduated, that website went back up.

That fall, I enrolled at LSU. Our website eventually became Studio8.net because my dorm room number was 8 and that's where all of our friends hung out.

A year later, I met a fella who was looking to get involved with comedy, Brock LaBorde, and we (along with our friends Matt, Alex, and Nathan) managed to get a sketch comedy show on LSU's *Tiger TV* on-campus TV station.

Brock and I started taking Studio8.net more seriously and it became a weekly satire newspaper, several self-produced parody albums, a feature film, internet sketches (four years before the term "web video" was ever invented), and a daily-updated comedy website.

Then we moved to New Orleans because the movie industry there had lots of fun jobs. I eventually heeded the advice of someone on the set of VH1's *Motormouth* and I took an improv class.

There, I met Tami Nelson and fell in love with improv and how comfortable it felt performing comedy with her.

That was 2004.

But Then...

In 2005, Hurricane Katrina hit New Orleans and we had to evacuate. It was the most devastating, heartbreaking experience of our lives - which feels ridiculous saying because we lost relatively very little in the hurricane.

However, our lives in the aftermath of Katrina were bittersweet.

We evacuated to Austin, Texas, directly after the storm and stayed there, partially because of the state of New Orleans, and partially because we saw an opportunity to cut our teeth on the American improv scene.

We spent the next year travelling to and performing at every improv festival we could. We had an opportunity to take classes and workshops with improv legends, see amazing shows, and become a part of a community that we were hungry to learn from, dissect, and explore.

Soon, back in Austin, we began teaching improv classes and opened an improv theater. Of course, we hardly knew what we were doing, but we were driven. We worked hard and believed in improv with our whole hearts, and even though we were fumbling through a million lessons about what not to do while running an improv theater, we were inspired.

Tami was the Conservatory Director of the theater, which pretty much meant: teach a shit load of Level 1 improv classes. Even though teaching several hours of Level 1 classes week after week can be exhausting and mentally warping, Tami was grateful for this time. It taught her to embrace the fundamentals, it reminded her week after week of how terrifying and freeing this art form is, it reinforced that there is magic on an improv stage, and most importantly, it taught her how to teach.

Now she craves teaching possibly more than she does performing.

Chris was the Artistic Director of the theater, which pretty much meant: book all the shows and produce special events. This was a lot of "non-creative" work, but Chris was grateful for this time, because an appreciation for executing a show from A to Z and maneuvering within other people's schedules were exactly the kinds of puzzles he liked tackling.

Now he loves producing almost as much as he loves performing.

In 2008, we focused up all of our ideas, philosophies, experiences, and goals and opened The New Movement in Austin. We immediately went on three tours - teaching workshops and tightening our syllabus.

In 2010, we expanded and opened up The New Movement in New Orleans.

In our spare time along the way, we helped launch The Dallas Comedy House in Dallas and The Station Theater in Houston.

After we'd had three years of nonstop teaching and performing under our belts, we learned one thing above all else: We have something to say about this.

So we started writing.

And Now...

And so we guess this book is what that is – the fruits of our writing labors.

Today, we can proudly say that both TNM theaters are thriving with beautiful, supportive communities of talented comedians and artists who stand together as one gigantic, mighty creative force that produces live comedy shows seven nights a week. TNM now has its own podcast network (TNM.fm); video, music, and print production arm (Studio 8), and year-round multi-city tours and festivals (Hell Yes Fest, Megaphone Marathons, the Improv Wins Conference, etc.).

We've lived and breathed improv with every ounce of our hearts and minds for the good part of a decade.

Improv has become so much more than a device of comedy. We believe in it.

Improv rules who we are and what we do on- and offstage.

Improv has taught us how to be better, smarter people.

Improv is love.

Sure, it's a cult.

But not all cults are bad…

CHAPTER 1

It's Not About the Dog

The stage is set!

Two brave improvisers jump onstage. They walk around the space for a moment, then to a spot where they meet and look at each other. They are moments into a scene and...they hesitate to initiate[1] with a line.

Time creeps along and both improvisers look at something on the ground.

And then, at last, one of them boldly creates an object.

Let's say that the object is a Dog. The two improvisers grasp tightly to this invention of Dog, steering all dialogue to the Dog for several lines.

The Dog is now a Fact.[2]

The two improvisers have agreed that this little bit of space on the stage is now being occupied by a Dog.

Done. Fact made.

Facts are comforting on our improv stage. The dog-as-fact has given the performers something to easily talk about. But the more they are talking about the dog, the more they are talking *about the dog*.

They are taking fewer risks with each line of dialogue that passes between them. They are speaking completely impersonally about

---

[1] Say ANYTHING to get your scene rolling. Pick a letter of the alphabet, choose a word that starts with that letter and start talking - "F"...ok...Fruit...ok...

"Fruit for sale! Sir, you look like you could use some fruit in your diet!"

And we're off! If played well, the scene will never be about the Fruit; it will be about these people in this space in time. Fruit just happens to occupy that same space.

[2] You can read more about Facts in Chapter 7!

this safe-ish non-thing. They have become isolated in a boring fact pile, most likely pretty detached from any sort of recognizable feeling.

And so it goes. The improvisers' dialogue winds along and they discover what kind of dog it is, what it does and doesn't do, etc., until at last, the two improvisers exhaust all the information about the dog and another improviser mercifully edits them.

Perhaps this scene got some chuckles because the improvisers are likable and their dialogue became a list of funny things about the dog: the dog is wearing a sweater, the dog is in sunglasses, the dog has an erection (beware the *list of funny things scene!*[3]).

Perhaps, and more likely, the improvisers both left the stage making faces that say, "That was kinda ok, I guess. How did we go wrong? The dog had an erection!"

This scene has happened a hundred-million-billlion times and will continue to appear on improv stages because its purpose is to teach us again and again that when we make our scenes *about the dog,* we are missing the point, we are not attaching to the improv.

In other words, the dog is a total emotional detachment.

So how do we fix it? Like with so many other questions regarding improv theories, the answer is incredibly simple, which makes it difficult.

"Emotion" is an inadequate word. When we tell our improv students to react *emotionally* to what's happening in the scene, our instruction is misrepresented by the word.

Emotion in improv is more than jealousy, hate, lust, joy. Rather, it's an all-encompassing multidimensional presence that the improviser assumes.

---

[3] The List of Funny Things Scene can become a shapeless, directionless, limp noodle of a scene that only gets rewarded with laughter because the players have managed to remain likable to the audience.

They're doing a scene about a dog...so they give it mange, they make it two-legged with a little wagon to drag itself around in, a cone head, humping/peeing/talking, etc. All of these listed things might get a laugh or two or ten, but ultimately they are just making a list of amusing things that could happen.

Rather than *showing* these funny things, we are *telling* them to the audience.

When an improviser is playing *emotionally*, they are aware of how they feel about themselves, the other players onstage, the situation they're in, and their intentions. They are para-emotional.

When we find we are entering into the danger zone of a scene being about the dog, we can re-route this scene by getting paranoid.

How do you feel about the other player?
How do you feel about the dog?
What does the dog mean to you about YOU?
What does this all mean to YOU about THEM?
What does this all mean to YOU about the situation?
Because the dog is here, are we unsafe or safer?
Does the dog make the other player kind or cold?

You just have to pick one![4]

---

[4] See also Chapter 6, concerning Paths - emotion as an element of relationship/dynamic.

Fight Club isn't about fighting.
It's about belonging!

Home Alone isn't about being home alone.
It's about appreciating and loving your family!

Air Bud: World Pup isn't about a golden retriever that plays soccer. It's about overcoming obstacles just like *Air Bud: Spikes Back* isn't about a golden retriever that plays volleyball! It, too, is all about overcoming obstacles[5]!

---

[5] The plot for *Air Bud: Spikes Back* goes like this: WARNING - SPOILER ALERT! *In Disney's fifth installment to the franchise, Air Bud realizes he can play beach volleyball. Throughout this experience, he and a talking parrot stop some crooks and make new friends. In the end, Air Bud goes to the championship and scores the winning spike.* We're not arguing against Air Bud as a talented athlete, but people can't be surprised at this point that the dude is good at <u>all sports</u>. If he's good at basketball and soccer, he's probably good at volleyball. Disney has earned the right to flip the pattern on us. What if Bud was also an expert marriage counselor? We can go on and on about this, but this chapter is not about the damn dog.

EXAMPLE TIME!

Brian and Jeff enter the scene and begin a dialogue about Jeff's dog. They discuss how the dog is sleeping, how the dog is lying in a puddle of water, how the dog is snoring weird snore sounds.

Jeff recognizes that he has been talking about the dog for five or six lines now, and a light bulb goes off in his head.

He thinks, *"The next thing that Brian says about the dog, I am going to react as if Brian just told me I won the lottery and I will have a huge emotional reaction."*

Brian tells Jeff that the dog looks like he's dead, and Jeff's entire body changes. He stands up super straight, he fist-pumps, he smiles, opens his eyes wide, and high-fives Brian.

Then he says, "Shit yeah, he looks like he's dead! Thanks for noticing! This is awesome!"

We have emotional attachment! Jeff now has a go-to for the rest of the scene - he knows that he is super-pumped that his friend finally noticed how dead his dog looks when it's sleeping.

If we apply our *"if this, then what"* tool to the scene, what other things are in this world that we can then see Jeff celebrate? And how does Brian feel about Jeff's reaction?

Let's say Brian decides to get on board with Jeff's emotional choice and mirrors a similar response.

Brian does a little dance, high-fives himself, and says "YES!" under his breath in triumph.

We don't know why these guys are so pumped about the dog looking dead, we just know that they 100% are.

We have a FACT in the scene that involves an emotional attachment.

If the dog wakes up, do both men fall into a sullen mood and act depressed?

What if we discover Jeff's girlfriend taking a nap on the couch?

Are they EVEN MORE excited about that because she's human?

This scene could go off in a number of different directions at this point, but as long as the two men commit to the emotion of the scene, they are likely to find much more interesting, funnier situations than if we never took the dog personally.

The above is definitely a weird example. But for a reason!

When newer improvisers learn to trust that ANYTHING can be interesting, they start to have better scenes faster.

Some improvisers think that if you throw enough backstory, exposition, pop culture references, funny phrases, or intelligent-sounding ideas at a scene, it will take shape the way they have it written in their heads.

However, if the improvisers trust that ANYTHING can be exalted, then we start to find our scenes taking more interesting shapes out of the first few moments of the scene.

The Dog can be a genius offer into the scene. Like any offer, it has meaning and weight. It serves as a tool to better understand the emotional moment in time that the improviser is in.

When we learn to listen to what emotional or para-emotional offer is being presented into the scene, we find our scenes opening more quickly to ideas and Paths that are not only more interesting and funny, but that are also simpler to follow.

When we are listing information about the dog, we have to think - our brain is busy churning, we are searching for the next piece of information - we are *acting*.

On the other hand, when we're engaged emotionally, we are *reacting* to the cues inside of ourselves, explanation becomes unnecessary, and we are no longer inventing information to explain why we're standing onstage.

There's a reason that so many spiritual practices focus on bringing you to the present moment. It's because the past (or that thing that doesn't *matter* right now, i.e. the dog) is no longer with us.

We learn from it, yes. But we don't live in it because the "here" affects who we are right now.

Know what I mean?

There are scenes that feel amazing, like you just made the world a better place by bringing that scene to life.

Those scenes are usually products of some kind of emotional investment. We gave something honest to the scene, exposed ourselves, or took a risk in that scene, made it real to us and relatable to our scene partners, and the audience responded positively.

And then there are those other scenes that feel like a cheap, half-drunk, one-night-stand with someone whose name you don't remember and who you couldn't recognize in a lineup.

We were detached, unemotional, desperate, and careless.

When we start to have some measure of success in improv, it's easy to phone it in, to pull from characters or scenarios you know will get laughs and just connect the dots.

But it kinda feels dirty.

We believe that becoming a better improviser is about being aware of this decision.

You *can* have meaningful relationship after meaningful relationship, just like you can string together a week's worth of one-night-stands.

Sure, both feel good, but which one makes you feel better?

PUT YOUR DOG TO THE QUIZ!

An improviser initiates a scene with the line, "Dad, I have to tell you something...I wrecked the car."

How should Dad respond?

    A) "My new car!?! I just bought that car!"

    B) "Well, I wrecked your bike, so we're even."

    C) "I am so proud of you, you're taking after your old man!"

The correct answer is "**C**"!

With the father being proud of his kid for wrecking the car, not only did he establish an emotional connection with the kid, but he also gave us an interesting absurd dynamic to play with. The scene has nothing to do with the car; the car is simply a symbol of their relationship.

So, what does the kid do now?

    A) Act surprised and call out that the Dad isn't mad.

    B) Proudly admit that not only did he wreck the car, but also he officially dropped out of high school.

    C) Act annoyed that he's anything like his Dad.

Totally choice "**B**", right?!

Since we now understand the dynamic behind father and kid, we can heighten and play with those facts.

Why would we want Dad to be mad? Dad was so proud a moment ago, let's make Dad MORE proud (heightening!).

Choices "**A**" and "**C**" are just further distancing Dad and Kid and skating close to an argument scene.

We are at our best in our scenes when we can see through all the dogs and the cars and the dance numbers and the taxicabs and make something - anything - have a personal meaning.

CHAPTER 2

Cats and Wrestling
(Use What You Know)

Let's say that you happen to have accidentally memorized the entire history of professional wrestling's Intercontinental Championship Belt or that you can comprehensively re-enact the climaxes of most WrestleMania main event matches.

Or let's say that you really like cats and you've known a lot of cool cats, so you happen to have a lot of cat behavior facts stored in your brain.

Now let's say that you're onstage and a situation arises, giving you the opportunity to showcase your encyclopedic feline knowledge.

Lucky you! It's now time for you to do one of our favorites things and that's Use What You Know!

Improv is heavy on the mental side.

We're listening, watching, supporting, directing, editing, acting, and writing all at once. When we add *inventing* to that list, it becomes more difficult to be present doing the above actions.

But when we *already know* the names of every Weezer album of all time[1] and it comes up in scene work, then it's time to have a little more fun.

Don't be shy. You know how many calories are in a Bobo's Peanut Butter Oat Bar, and since we're talking about snacking right in the second beat of this Harold, go ahead and say it - 190 calories per serving, two servings per container.

Cedar Waxwings are birds that notoriously snack on fermented berries, which makes them "drunk" and so they do crazy un-birdlike things, like fly into your house and try to hangout with you.

---

[1] *Blue, Pinkerton, Green*. That's it.

Hey, that's great inspiration for this scene where we're all playing different animals!

You know that the Jazz is a weird name for a professional basketball team in Utah and that the Jazz name never should have left its former team name home in New Orleans, so since we're talking about names that don't feel right, it might be fun to drop that nugget of knowledge, too!

So long as the Branch doesn't outweigh the Tree, we're golden (Chapter 5 of this book talks a lot more about this!).

Sometimes the most powerful comedy comes from the information stored inside of your specific unique brain.

That information is relatable to the audience in some ways, sure, but more importantly, when you are speaking from a place of 100% confidence in your knowledge, you are telling the audience, "I've got this," which is what they came to see in the first place.

The most uncomfortable moments in an improv theater are when we (the audience and players) are watching someone be self-conscious and self-doubtful onstage.

Everyone in that room wants you to succeed!

They want you to nail this!

Most people don't come to improv shows to be judgmental; they're here to laugh!

That's a really great support system for this totally scary art form, so take care of yourself and show them what you've got.

You just got endowed as a biologist, but you know nothing about science - but you *do* know a lot about *feng shui*.

Great!

Now you are the biologist who is constantly rearranging his lab to have the most zen-like atmosphere!

Good job! You just Yes, And-ed your scene partner and took care of yourself by embracing their idea and giving yourself a voice with which to speak throughout the scene. Plus, that *feng shui*-obsessed biologist character is probably way more interesting than just a straight up normal biologist guy.

Play what you know, play what you have thought about from a number of different angles inside and out, and then show us!

EXAMPLE TIME!

Here's an exercise you can do by yourself in your room or while riding on a bus full of strangers. Pick one thing from column A and another from column B and think of a good initiating line!

Column A You've just been endowed as...	Column B You happen to know a lot about...
• A caged rabbit • Jackie Chan • Talking piece of bubblegum[2] • Jake the Snake Roberts • Tommy Wiseau • The best Jamaican tour guide there is • Personal Injury Attorney Bart Morris	• Credit card debt • Making soups • Bath salts • The 2002 *MTV Spring Break* programming schedule • Colorado Springs • Growing up in a three-story house • Zebras[3]

So, for example, the Jamaican Tour Guide can make up facts about Jamaica, or since he's really from Colorado (like you), he can guide the scene towards that. The tour guide is absurd and the people expecting some history about Jamaica are straight.

"It doesn't get very cold in Jamaica. Nothing like Colorado Springs, at least! One winter, I was with my friends and we were hanging out at Pike's Peak and you'll never believe what happened next..."

---

[2] Fruit Stripes Gum scenes RULE.
[3] Fruit Stripes Gum scenes RULE.

Remember, just because you've been endowed as something you know very little about doesn't mean that you're in a bad place. The tree trunk is only beginning to form.

It usually happens at the end of a Level 1 improv class. People start to feel a little more comfortable with each other, start to make more daring offers, start to show their true selves a little more.

This is when we start to see the Civil War scenes.

One dude in class just happens to know a shit-ton of American Civil War facts, so he initiates a scene as General Robert E. Lee.

Even if no one else in class has studied the Civil War since high school, we all see the glimmer in The General's eyes, we all know that he will protect and guide us, we know that That Dude Has Got This, and we trust the scene.

Of course, this scene is never going to hug too tightly to actual historical facts. It will instead be peppered throughout the scene (which actually becomes something more akin to a Straight/Absurd Everything-Goes-Wrong-At-General-Lee's-Battle scene than anything else) with interesting Civil War facts, which delights the Civil War aficionado and also entertains the lay audience member.[4]

The Civil War is simply a framework over which we throw a veil or filter. We understand the basic events and details that exist on the battlefield, we have soldiers and weapons and maps and strategies. All of the players can agree to The Facts of this framework.

The thing that makes this scene interesting is the filter through which we play the framework.

If the filter is "General Lee is a lovesick romantic," we play through all of the things that would exist in the framework of "Civil War Battle" with that filter on it.

---

[4] If you find yourself in the Civil War scene and you can't remember actual war facts, give yourself a relationship!
Be General Lee's super dorky brother!
Swoon every time a new soldier speaks!
Be the camp cook who thinks he's better than everyone and makes gourmet blue corn fritters and white beans with pistou!

The sound of explosions in the distance reminds him of his first kiss with his true love, the crinkle of the map makes him swoon because it reminds him of his sweetheart's petticoats, etc.

We can confidently navigate this scene because The Framework of the scene is relatable.

Confidence begets trust, and trust makes it easier for us to take risks with each other - and that's where so many of the pay-offs come from in improv.

Whenever we do anything with confidence, we are communicating volumes more than just, "I know a lot about cats."

We are saying to our fellow improvisers and to the audience, "I am totally allowing myself to have fun showing who I am to everyone right now."

We think the audience will love you for it.

CHAPTER 3

Do Not Open The Box
(Narrative, Editing, Beats)

For a lot of people, editing an improv scene is really simple. You wait until the scene cannot possibly get any funnier and then you gallop across the stage.

For some, though, editing is a nightmare.

Some of us pick up bad habits early in our improv training and we perpetuate them by holding back and not following our feet.

Since the overall success of your scene can be measured by the timing of your edit, let's review.

Late Edits

Late edits make us feel like the strong winds that have been blowing our ship's sails have abruptly died down from a mighty gust to a sad little cough.

When an edit is missed, everyone feels it.

The improvisers onstage start to panic, attempting to keep their scene afloat, the cast on the wings frantically hang onto every line for anything that can be an edit, the audience shifts in their seats - not knowing exactly what has happened, but knowing that something has gone wrong (after all, all the scenes before this one were so wonderful!).

Most of the time, we know exactly when to edit - when the improvisers onstage have heightened the scene to a lofty crescendo, when the game has been played out and the pattern satisfied, when The Thing we've been waiting for in the scene is about to happen, that's when we know to edit.

Sometimes, throughout the entire scene, we have anticipated some BIG THING to happen. We've played four or five minutes into the scene, and we know it's time for *The Thing*:

- At last the new boss will open the weird present from corporate!

- Finally, the camper will read the letter from Grandpa!

- The shopkeeper will close the shop and the irritating customer will have no other choice but to leave!

We are taught in our improv classes that we should play this scene right up to the point of when The Thing is about to happen and then edit, leaving the scene to float off into the ether with the audience and performers forever not knowing the outcome of The Thing.

It is important to understand why we learn this.

It's bigger than just timing.

It's more than just scene pacing and heightening.

It's all about truly embracing the ephemeral nature of this art form, being comfortable with simply creating trajectory, establishing an emblem of an idea with the intention of casting it from ourselves in celebration of its impermanence.

It's also, for whatever reason, funnier[1].

If we let the boss go ahead and open the box, we are breaking the delicate threads that hold the precarious structure of this art form together when the edit doesn't come at Minute Five of the scene, when the boss is *just about* to open the box.

What makes this even more uncomfortable is that the boss just got a big laugh before he picked up the box, which, as we'll soon discover, should have been the edit point.

So he opens the weird present from corporate, and against his best judgment, he helplessly and desperately utters a line *that could never be as interesting as we need it to be to be right now* - the bubble bursts, the scene folds in on itself, and all that is left to look forward to in this scene is an awkward late edit.

When we have worked so thoughtfully and diligently to build tension in the scene, <u>that is what the scene is about</u> - it only exists to build tension never to be released, the "problem" never to be solved, but only to be made "worse."

---

[1] Another way of approaching this: A good improv audience wants to be in on the fun. They want to think they can figure out where we're going with this stuff. The perfect edit will create fantastical post-show conversations like, "I wonder why that present made him vomit?"
This is an improv sweet spot: performers loving their work and audience members loving the performers. Improv Wins!

The scene is solely about all of the things that happen when we don't know what's in the weird gift from corporate, it's not about what the gift is (and it's not about the Dog, either).

Releasing tension and opening the gift is an introduction of narrative, which some folks try to achieve in improv.

A narrative, however, has a path that only exists through new invention, exploring *forward,* which is very difficult for people to agree to do on an improv stage.

Moving forward together successfully in a scene is more easily achieved when we are heightening facts that we have already agreed upon in our scene.

We agree that This Gift Came From Corporate.

We agree that It Is Weird.

If we explore those facts, we are more likely to be on the same page, finding ideas and establishing patterns together, and therefore working forward with the same toolboxes.

If we have to make new inventions to achieve story arch and a sensible conclusion, we are working with a far less stable base of information, inventing new information, rather than shoring up agreed upon facts.

It is totally all about the journey.[2]

---

[2] See also: The road trip is more fun than the destination. The flirting was better than the sex. The construction of (and bragging about) the world's largest laser bomb was more satisfying than actually destroying the planet.

When we open the box, we have to deal with what is in the box.

Before this, the scene was all about not dealing with what was in the box, but was instead exploring all of the circumstances that surround the box:

☑ How does the new boss feel about getting the gift?

☑ What does it mean that corporate sent the gift?

☑ How do the other co-workers feel about the gift/the boss/corporate?

We look at what elements are driving the scene and that is our Path - if the GIFT itself is driving our scene, then it's possible our scene is a flat, energy-less, list-of-funny-things scene.

It's more fun to be in an oh-my-gosh, what-does-this-mean-in-the-here-and-now scene.

When we as improvisers truly understand that the journey is the solitary goal, edits become easier, their timing gets clearer, and we have moments when everyone from the wings edits the scene at the same time because everyone knew the precise moment to do so.

And because our scene was edited at just the right moment (when our sails were at their fullest and we were cruising faster than ever), we are so close to The Perfect Scene.[3]

Early Edits
(see also Chapter 4 for lots more about this!)

A scene edited too soon feels like finding out that the person you had a crush on all throughout high school totally had a hardcore crush on you, too (Oh, what could have been!?!).

Beginning improvisers study scenes to learn how to <u>recognize</u> The Game[4].

However, mastering how to play it is another skill altogether. Early edits are usually the result of an improviser recognizing that a Beat or two of a Game has been established and they panic and edit.

Let's review **Beats** (vocab alert)!

Beats are a measure of Game in the scene. Beats in improv are not time units, they are rather semi-structured segments that define and progress The Game of the scene.

---

[3] The first note that a non-improviser who watches a lot of shows will give to their improviser friend is that "they should have edited that sooner."
They are, unfortunately, usually right.

[4] Has anyone ever taught a workshop on Game and insisted on being introduced to the students while pro wrestler HHH's intro music blasted? (It IS how you play the game…)
PS – This footnote is for hardcore wrestling fans only.

We say the comedic "Rule of Three" applies to Beats, but it's rather the "Rule of <u>At Least</u> Three."

Within a Beat, a Pattern may be established.

Beat one sets up the potential Game, potential Pattern.

Beat two solidifies that this is now The Game and Pattern.

Beat three and beyond serve to heighten the elements of this Game.

The Game is the structure that drives the scene, maintaining the Pattern is a bonus. The harder you play the Pattern, the more specific your scene becomes, increasing the potential for mad success later in the scene.

EXAMPLE TIME!

<u>Beat One:</u> Alex Woodward and Chris Sherrod are co-workers at lunch, eating sandwiches.
Alex complains about how he bruised his knee and feels like he should take a sick day.
Chris responds, telling Alex that a bruised knee is hardly a big deal and he should just work through it.

<u>Beat Two:</u> Justin Strackany joins the lunchroom scene and starts eating chips.
He complains that he has a paper cut and feels like he really needs to go on sick leave.
Chris responds with confusion, and repeats the sentiment that this is a minor injury. Chris is acting as what has now been defined as a straight character.

<u>Beat Three:</u> Christy Lorio joins the lunchroom and sips from a water fountain.
She announces that she failed P.E. in high school and thinks she should get disability relief from the government.
Chris is baffled, frustrated, and tells everyone that these are ridiculous claims, and he reminds them that last year he wore a neck brace to work for three weeks and never took a sick day.

This is a super simplistic example of how we can clearly heighten an idea by grabbing the first unusual idea in the scene and defining it through Beats.

The first Beat introduces a potential game - an illness that is not at all severe that's being treated as if it is.

The following Beats don't have to be so specifically married to Beat One as illustrated in this example – with all offerings from other performers being different types of "ailments."

The pattern in this example – again, extremely simplistic – was what they consumed when they entered the scene. The less severe the illness of each character, the less they consumed.

So by this pattern, we know that if someone was to enter the scene who had broken both of their arms, they would definitely be eating a steak, another character that was even less injured than Christy would possibly just scrape bits of crumbs from their shirt and eat that.

Breaking this pattern at any point won't kill the scene, but sticking to the pattern through the end will send it through the roof and into the stars while safely wrapped in bubbles and rainbows.

Beats can heighten the overall concept of "first bit of information in a scene."

Using our "if this, then what" approach, we can follow different possible pattern paths. If bruised knee equals something not bad that's treated as if it's really bad, then what else is like that?

- ☑ A flat tire = I need a new car.
- ☑ Girlfriend didn't call back = You'll never have children.
- ☑ News reported gas prices on the rise = You should move to Central America.

The longer it takes to establish "The Thing[5]" or "The Game of the scene," the more likely your scene will be sliced in half with an edit, especially if your troupe has yet to establish any group mind.

Many new improvisers will take "back-having" too far and put any scene "out of its misery" if it seems slow right out of the gate.

Others will feel it's okay to edit quickly because "you could always go back to that scene," which is completely true. Also completely true is that this only happens 12% of the time.[6]

The better we know our fellow performers, the better we'll be able to make assumptions like, "It took them a while to find the Game, but now they've got it and I'll give them time to heighten."[7]

---

[5] **True Stories with Christopher Michael:** I've done three comedy shows in Tucson, AZ, and I've been to The Thing three times. If you don't know what The Thing is, then you should travel through Tucson on I-10.

[6] We totally made this stat up but it *feels* real.

[7] And if you're a veteran improviser performing with a bunch of rookie improvisers, they'll (unfortunately) give you ten minutes to discover and play the game.

"Edit" the Dog

For more on edits, we'd like to introduce our pal, Edit the Dog![8]

Edit is a real good dog. She listens intently and is very loyal to her owner, Improv. Edit is energetic when she needs to be, and calm and cool when she doesn't. She understands that even when she is not in the scene, she is still in the show. When Edit does a good job, we all make sure she knows by rubbing her tummy and feeding her snacks.

Let's follow Edit as she demonstrates her favorite things to do!

---

[8] "Edit" is a Pembroke Welsh Corgi, the smartest dog in the Herding Group. There are lots of videos online of Corgis sleeping on their backs!

Edit closely watches the scene, listening to every word.

Edit doesn't get in prime running position. She doesn't call any attention to herself because she's not in this scene.

The scene is over and Edit jogs across the stage when the time is right.
The audience claps! Good girl!

If Edit were not paying attention, she could miss a key word.

Edit is in position to end the scene OR employ a device. She
understands that timing is everything.

If she runs real fast across the stage,
it might be distracting.

If she walks too slowly, it might
feel like she's Walking On.

So she listens closely and then jogs just right!

Edit is waiting for an edit point in the scene.

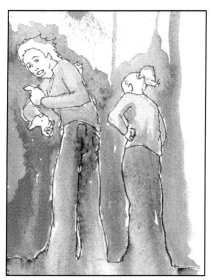

The person onstage calls for an edit.

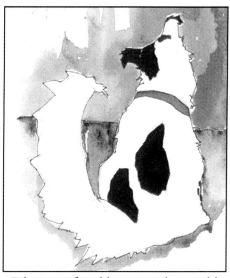

Edit is confused because why would someone do this?

Edit makes eye contact with someone on the other side.

The other person starts to edit as Edit does.

They meet in the middle and begin a scene.

A Few More Thoughts on Edits

Dennis Rodman

We don't think that The Worm ever did improv (Southeastern Oklahoma State didn't offer the course), but if he did, we bet he'd be pretty good at editing.

While playing professional basketball from 1986-2000, Dennis Rodman built up a reputation for being the game's best rebounder. While grabbing boards won't net you much off-court glamour, the five-time NBA Champion made it into an art.

On a similar note, editing won't get you on the cover of Improv Monthly[9], but you'll carve out a reputation for yourself if you keep your eye on the ball and stay in position to make a play.

If Dennis Rodman did want to take some classes, we recommend his hometown's Dallas Comedy House, which is located about 94 miles away from his college.

Everyone's Job Is To Edit

If you're not in the scene, you should be listening closely for the edit.

If you're in the scene and your partners on the sidelines miss an edit, then you should take it upon yourself to edit.

It's not as pretty, but it's much better looking than cooking.

Anyone who's ever said the words, "That scene would have been so much better if someone would have edited it," should instead start saying, "That scene would have been so much better if I would have just edited it myself."

Real talk.

---

[9] At the time of this printing, *Improv Monthly* does not actually exist. If you want to make that happen, this is a free idea - a gift from us to you.
All we ask in return is that you also syndicate The Adventures of Edit.

Don't Walk Slow or Run Fast

If you've been doing improv for a while with the same group of people, you have likely figured out what speed works for you.

For those of you who are still working on this, listen up.

Don't run so fast across the stage that you have to stop yourself from knocking over a wall, and don't walk so slow that your friends onstage aren't sure if you're walking on or editing.

Both are weird and we don't want you to look or feel weird, because we like you a lot.

There Are Brains In Your Legs

How many times have you started to edit a scene, changed your mind, didn't edit it, and then you soon regretted it?

What many improvisers don't realize is that our legs have tiny computers in them called brains and these brains only have ears and no eyes, and they know exactly when the scene is over.

That jump we feel in our lower half is our body urging us to jog across the stage.

It's begging us to trust its judgment.

When we don't trust it, our entire body flinches, and when our body flinches, we draw attention to it, and when the audience sees that we've seen a missed edit, the curtain falls from the ceiling and covers up all the disappearing magic.

QUIZ: THE ULTIMATE EDIT!

We've nailed our scenes and we've treated each other like geniuses and now it's time for it to come to an end.

It's been twenty-four minutes and Sam Stites just initiated a scene with all the parents in the neighborhood, each of whom has a clever something to say.

It's perfect.

Even better, Sam has a brilliant line that not only makes complete sense in this current context, but it's the world's smoothest callback to the beginning of the show.

The only problem is, the intern in the light booth is drawing circles on a piece of scratch paper and the edit was – *gasp!* – missed.

Here's a quiz:

What do the performers do now?

A) Continue on with the scene and then hold a grudge against the intern in the booth.

B) Wave your hands wildly in the "and the lights come down" motion until the intern notices and makes the lights come down.

C) Reference the missed edit point repeatedly in your scene work until the intern wakes up.

D) Jump out of the scene and exclaim to the audience, "Thank you, that's been our show!"

The only answer here is **D**.

Ending the show yourself is not ideal for many people (most often the kind of people who actively avoid introducing the troupe at the top of the show, as it's the real you), but in situations like this, it's the best solution.

All of the other above quiz choices have actually happened to us before and have resulted in both the performers and the audience leaving the show with an awkward taste in their mouths.

And awkwardness tastes really weird, leaving the audience with a weird taste in their mouths.[10]

---

[10] And let's face it, that's pretty awkward.

CHAPTER 4

Make the Scene Buy You a Drink[1]
(Heightening, Some Straight/Absurd, Funniest Choices, Multiply Laughs)

Badass.

Look at how far we've come!

We have advanced in our improv training.

We have been practicing improv for a while, have taken a few levels of classes and some workshops, and have traveled to see shows in other cities.

We have had at least one improv epiphany - that moment onstage, in class, in the shower, or on the bus - when all of a sudden a thunderclap happens, a single strand of light illuminates, and the holographic improv clouds part in our brains and we think, "Oh, THAT'S what THAT is!!!"

We're truly studying comedy, and now, at least intellectually, we can understand beats, patterns, and heightening.

We have started to fall in love with improv. And it feels right - butterflies and champagne bubbles.

And then something remarkable starts happening.

---

[1] One day in class, Tami was leading a discussion about scene pacing, and one of her delightful students, Margaux Binder, said, "You should make the scene buy you a drink."

Tami loved it and said, "I'm going to use that."

Margaux said, "OK, cool."

And here we are.

The majority of our scenes are good; they feel good, they are well received, and they are smart and funny. *We* are smart and funny. We are good looking, confident and interesting. People talk to us about our scenes after our shows or classes, and they look at us like they're thinking, "To me, you are magic."

And this is exciting!

Perhaps too exciting...because now we find ourselves being tempted to act like an overwhelmed, horny teenager who turns a simple kiss into an opportunity to go all the way.

Just when we're starting to actually get some action, we go and screw it all up by being monstrously aggressive, and prematurely ejaculate all over our scenes.

The mature improviser knows how ultimately unsatisfying this can be, but they also know how to turn what looks like a one-night stand into a lasting, loving relationship.

In an improv sense, at least.

They know that a good scene needs some romance, flirtation, and a few drinks before we even get to the big-ticket business.

They know that together we will build up to the good stuff, and we will reach the golden ceiling of ultimate scene work, but that we can't get there by rushing to it.

Only pacing, patience, trust, and focus will get us there.

EXAMPLE TIME!

It's a classic first date scene...

Jessica Brown and Brady James sit across from each other, making small talk and flirty, nervous gestures.

Once we have The Framework of "date" established, Jessica starts to discuss in gross detail her past sexual experiences with her last boyfriend.

Brady responds to this by acting curious about this absurd character. *Why would she bring this up on a date?* And he starts to practice his newly learned skills as a Straight Man.

He goes to his "Emotion Wheel[2]" and paces out his reactions with a nice range of non-aggressive emotions: Suspicion, Nervousness, Curiosity, Disbelief, etc.

This scene is set up beautifully - a classic straight/absurd scene.

If we give this scene room to breathe, it can develop and earn four or five minutes of giddy laugh-filled moments as we slowly reveal how nuts-o this girl character is.

Jessica and Brady know this.

They are looking at each other across the "table" and they know, as improvisers, what they have stumbled upon...

They remember lectures from class about The Straight/Absurd Dynamic, and at last, they understand it as it unfolds before them...

They are seeing the codes of The Matrix everywhere...

Do they know what to do next?

YES!

...and then...Jessica goes from lengthy, detailed descriptions of her ex-boyfriend's sexual habits to pulling out a gun.

---

[2] Check out the Emotion Wheel in Chapter 7!

She jumps from A to B, then suddenly to Z, and somebody quickly edits the scene, thinking that it can't be heightened any further.

She got one tiny kiss and then she ripped off her clothes[3].

If Jessica had wrapped up the conversation about her ex's weird sexual habits and then reigned it in for a moment (returning to the Trunk[4] of the scene, which was "Awkward First Date"), perhaps asking what Brady likes to do on the weekends, she could milk the uneasy and strange tension of their established dynamic through every possible "offering" in the scene.

Once we have a fairly clear map of heightening in our scenes, we can take our time and explore all the twists and turns and details of the map.

As Brady discusses why he enjoys going to baseball games on the weekends (because his father, who recently passed away, used to take him every weekend - heightening Brady's straight character and Making It Worse[5]), Jessica is simply making a face of pure ecstasy and precisely lining all the plates up in a row in front of her, occasionally closing her eyes and licking her lips.

----

[3] Sure, this could end up being a decent one-night stand or an okay scene in a show where we are intentionally going for quick scenes, but we're trying to build something stronger here.

[4] See Chapter 5 for more on Trunks!

[5] Make it worse! Our rational mind tells us to be nice to our scene partners. We have to override that instinct to be nice and helpful and learn that what feeds many improv scenes is making "it" worse.

It is SO MUCH MORE uncomfortable to be on an awkward date with someone who is talking about raunchy sex stuff while you're regaling them with memories of your dead father. That discomfort for the characters in the improv scene can equal major giggles for the audience!

This way, Jessica is taking every opportunity in the scene to heighten the absurdity she has established for herself. Brady is taking every opportunity in the scene to heighten her absurdity, too.

Jessica has found a clear way to say to Brady, "Psst! I am playing a totally absurd character, so let's show all the ways I can creep you out!"

At the same time, Brady strengthens his own character, giving attributes to himself that will heighten the absurdity of Jessica's character.

Jessica continues talking about how many boyfriends she has had and all of their weird sexual habits.

Brady offers that he's only had a few relationships and they were all very serious and he never talks about sex on a first date.

By making the choice to define this as a first date, Brady has helped to heighten Jessica's character.

The tricky thing is, Brady needs to avoid making the scene about any of these individual moves of the girl - it's not about her weird sex talk or lining up plates - we don't dare call these details out.

That's playing Word Association[6], which can hamper the strength of our scenes.

When we can trust that "we" (us and our fellow improvisers) are all seeing the same map (or if not *exactly* the same, a very similar idea and outline) of the scene, we can relax.

Advanced improvisers have built up this skill in themselves through experience. They know that once Brady has confessed some touching story about the last baseball game that he and his dad went to, then Jessica will take inspiration from some element of the baseball story and begin to heighten her character again (and vice-versa!).

---

[6] Seriously: See Chapter 5. It's the next chapter after this one, ya big lug!

Once Jessica has set her absurdity into motion, Brady - as the straight character - can then look for opportunities to set her up to show the audience new facets of her absurdity.

If he knows that she is overtly and excruciatingly sexualizing things in the scene, it becomes his job to make offers to the scene that will exploit this fact in interesting, intelligent ways.

But what is the funniest choice?

Is it funnier to order Jessica a plate of sausage (we know exactly what to expect when she gets a plate full of sausages) or is it funnier to show her the sentimental Donald Duck wristwatch that your dad left you when he passed away?

As audience members, we've probably all seen the "sausage blowjob scene" before, but we haven't seen the "sexualized wristwatch" one.

How will she filter this information of Dad's old watch through her sexualized character!?!

Both improvisers can take the risk to make this a more interesting, less predictable choice because they both trust that Jessica knows to somehow sexualize the heirloom, heightening the absurdity of her character.

With each offer like this that Brady makes to Jessica, the pair are multiplying the laughter of the scene, they are giving the audience what they want, and together - the improvisers and the audience - they are building towards the great crescendo – a mighty roar of laughter, thundering applause, and an edit.

The scenario described above isn't far-fetched. If you've been doing improv for a couple of months, chances are you've encountered a completely absurd character.

How often have you fed the monster? It's easy for Brady to sit back and let Jessica take control of the scene. It's a lot more fun to play alongside her, though.

We want to be kissed all over our bodies before we even think about taking off our clothes. We want to linger and be patient and let the tension build. It's super difficult to trust that we are reading each other's minds onstage - but it's not impossible.

If we just relax and focus and let the scene happen, we can milk it for every possible laugh.

How to Make the Funniest Choice

Asking improvisers to make the "funniest choice" is a vague note.

What is funny?

What will the audience think is funny?

There is no measure for what is funnier, but there is a measure for what is less funny.

Good news! What's funnier is vastly broader than what is not.

The simplest possible explanation is that the funniest choices are always the least expected ones. At its most basic, that's what a punchline is - an unexpected button at the end of a setup.

These choices are most successful when they come from the unique voice of the honest improviser. When the improviser is making choices in the scene that they personally and honestly are inspired by, that they believe in, then they are more likely to communicate something funny to the audience.

Let's say that you know a lot about animals[7]. You can reference species names in Latin and all that. It is 100% fact that you will get a bigger laugh from the audience by giving us jokes filtered through your hyper-extensive biological classification character than through the dude that tells dick jokes like he's Andrew Dice Clay.

Because we've seen the Diceman before. We've already laughed at that.

But we haven't ever seen YOU as THAT annoying species-identifying character.

The element of surprise - giving the audience something they've never seen - wins over the improv crowd every time. It feeds the energy that exists in the improv show.

We as improvisers don't know what to expect because we've never done this show before...so give them (the audience) something they've never seen.

---

[7] In case you forgot, we happen to know a lot about Cats & Wrestling.

CHAPTER 5

Rely on the Trunk, Beware of the Branch

The trunk is the main structural member of the tree. From the trunk grow the branches. Over time, the trunk strengthens and becomes a tall and mighty tree.

Branches, however, are often found lying broken on the ground or thrown in a campfire. There are many uses for branches, but it's important to note that with no trunk there is no branch, and no branch is as large as the tree. You can climb a tree and venture out onto a branch, but unless you jump (dangerous!), you're coming back down the trunk.

It's easy to get distracted during an improv scene. In addition to the many factors involved with maintaining the scene itself, there are bright lights and video cameras and good-looking people in the audience/class watching your every move.

And in the scene, there are characters and dynamics and tangents and object work and accents, as well as a million subliminal messages being sent across the stage all at once.

We are expected to navigate all of these different signals and stay focused in our scenes, but sometimes we get lost along the way and find ourselves waaaaaaay out on a limb.

In order to climb to the top of the tree (where the best view is, the Perfect Scene), we must avoid the temptations of camping out on the branches[1].

---

[1] Don't be fooled by Word Association - it will often lead you down a path that makes sense for a short while, but those branches aren't built to hold all that weight

We can wander out on a branch for a little while, but in order to heighten, we must return to the trunk to climb.

The trunk and branches grow from the roots of the scene. The roots are the things that hold the trunk in place - a solid relationship.

Even if the characters in the scene are strangers, they still have a relationship. They have feelings towards each other; they have parameters in which they behave with one another.

What they choose to do with those feelings and parameters then becomes the Trunk of our scene.

How they play their feelings, relationship parameters, and/or Framework is what inspires our Branches.

The Trunk contains all of the truth and emotional reactions that protect our scene and give it life. It's a constant that organically grows and spawns Branches, but our obligation as climbers is to stay the course.

Example 1:
TRUNK: I'm leaving you.
BRANCH #1: You never did the dishes.
BRANCH #2: I've met somebody else.
BRANCH #3: You can keep the kids.

The branches serve as examples that further illustrate the trunk of the scene. The trunk of the scene is "I'm leaving you," so we should never veer too far from that.

Let's look at another example using this same premise, one that falls into the Word Association trap.

---

for too long and suddenly - snap! - the branch and the scene break. Stick to the trunk and make your job as an improviser easier.

Example 2:
TRUNK: I'm leaving you.
BRANCH #1: You never did the dishes.
BRANCH #1A: I don't like doing the dishes.
BRANCH #1A*: Neither do I, but I always did them.
BRANCH #1A**: You should have told me about the dishes.
BRANCH #1A***: I shouldn't have to, the dishes are right there in the sink.

This scene is not about the dishes, but it became about the dishes because we camped out on the dishes branch and stayed there.

Creating branches is a helpful tactic to fill out space and give color and depth to your scene, but should never take the focus away. It's never about the dishes, the dog, the weird gift from corporate, etc.

Now, here's a slightly more complex example that utilizes the strength of branches.

Example 3:
TRUNK: I want to sleep with you.
BRANCH #1: Let's order another round of drinks.
BRANCH #1A: If I drink, I won't be able to drive home.
BRANCH #1B: What kind of car do you drive?
BRANCH #1C: Buick Park Avenue.
TRUNK: That's so sexy.
BRANCH #2: Should we order dessert?
BRANCH #2A: The chocolate mousse looks good.
TRUNK: It's probably all soft...and moist.

Even when we're talking about the car and the dessert in our branches, we're still talking about lust (the trunk). This creates an easy-to-follow Pattern that will not only serve the rest of *this* scene, but any scene that follows it that mentions a car or dessert[2].

---

[2] Let's say that two scenes later we see a scene between two people stuck in traffic. An easy callback and walk-on (or drive-on) in this scene could be another driver pulls up

Our two players can now boldly venture out onto a variety of different branches - politics, family secrets, philosophy, technology, religion. They can be detailed and variegated, as long as they every-so-often return to heightening the lust.

Maintaining a strong trunk is essential to any improv scene. It's both something to hold onto and something to come back to.

---

beside them and asks is they're driving a Buick Park Avenue. When the driver responds that it is, of course the other driver is super turned on and speeds away.

Complications and Confusion with Word Association

We've devoted an entire chapter to Word Association (Chapter 8), but since it's really important to us that you don't do it, we wanted to pre-mention it here in big font that will hopefully capture your attention and burn it into your brain.

Word Association is dangerous because it leads us down a path without a map.

When we are wandering from one reference to the next, it's more difficult to heighten a scene, thus making our scene less editable, thus putting us at risk of losing momentum in our scene, which puts us at risk of thinking too hard about what to do to save the scene, which takes us out of the moment, which threatens our listening, which means we are no longer attached to our scene partner, which means we have no roots to our scene.

Grody.

52

CHAPTER 6

Paths and Weapons
The Perfect Scene/Minimalist Improv

Every improv scene starts out perfect.

However, most scenes soon lose momentum because the improviser over-complicates their craft.

The trick is to choose your Path and Weapon and then carry the Perfect Scene from start to finish.

Paths: Relationship, Premise, Character, Dynamic, Game

There are elements that naturally accompany our Paths.

Identifying with an emotion, for example, is going to define the relationship.

Making a strong character choice will communicate your point of view.

Initiating a Game gives everyone a dialogue/editing pattern to follow.

The Perfect Scene contains multiple combinations of these elements, but never all of them. That clever "just bring one brick, not a wheelbarrow full" line we heard as improv babies still applies.

Let's see what happens when we concentrate on one of these elements, nail it, and then mix in the others as needed.

The easiest scenario to demonstrate here is a Character scene. When a Character shines in a scene, the Setting will organically fill itself in, so the need to create one becomes less important.

A tough-guy cowboy gets off his horse.

A talkative auto-mechanic lifts the hood.

A nervous coach takes a knee and calls his team over.

It doesn't really matter where he is or what her name is. It only matters that he/she exists and is doing whatever he/she does. The Setting fills itself in.

The Path has been decided. Now choose your Weapon.

Weapons: Pattern, Setting[1]

Your Weapon helps spotlight what's funny about the scenario. Sure, we can have funny characters in crazy premises - and yes those scenes can be really awesome.

When we're talking about The Perfect Scene through Paths and Weapons, though, we are striving for the strongest, most interesting, hilarious, and most clearly mapped-out scenes.

If Mr. and Mrs. Price (Relationship) are discussing their crippling financial woes while getting a couple's massage at a fancy resort, then the Setting is your Weapon.

When Mr. Price announces that they cannot afford to pay their car note, Mrs. Price orders another banana daiquiri.

And when he gets a text message from his bank saying that his account has overdrawn, Mrs. Price responds by tipping 50%.

Our selection of Relationship and Setting has now led us to a Pattern or Game.

---

[1] When we say "Setting," we mean the environment, time of day, location, etc.

EXAMPLE TIME!

When Jared tells the girl behind the deli counter, Hillary, that he wants a pound of roast beef, and Sean Brightman tells her that he wants a new job, we're looking at either a Straight/Absurd Dynamic or a Character scene.

- If we embrace the differences between Jared and Sean (roast beef vs. new job), then we're likely to be heading down the Dynamic Path with a Setting Weapon.

- If we end up tapping out Jared with his roast beef, we've chosen to follow the path of Sean's job-wanting Character and now all energies are focused on making Sean as weird/inappropriate/depressed as possible. (Hint: Pick an adjective and get to work!) This is a Character Path with the Tap-Outs creating new Settings.

- If the scene evolves to become "Every time Jared orders something, Sean confesses that he wants to change part of his life," then we've combined Character with Game and Pattern.

- If Michael taps in and puts Sean in a psychologist's office and asks him what's been troubling him, and he replies with "BLT, no mayo", then we've got ourselves a hilarious, immediate Edit!

ANOTHER EXAMPLE TIME!

Lindsay Adkins thinks she's locked her phone and keys in her car.

Chadwick Smith, a complete stranger, walks by on his phone, notices, and expresses his desire to help.

Lindsay says that he can actually help her by calling a locksmith over.

Chadwick claims that his phone is out of battery, though, so Lindsay is out of luck.

Randy walks up next and also wishes he could help.

Lindsay says that he can, as he's carrying a jacket on a wire hanger.

However, that jacket is for a meeting that Randy is running late to, so Lindsay is again, out of luck.

Finally, Megan approaches the car.

Before Lindsay can say a word, Megan unlocks the door, gets in, and drives away.

It wasn't Lindsay's car after all.

Edit.

Note all the Paths and Weapons that weren't pinnacle to this scene:
- Setting (Where were they? What time was it? What time period was it?)
- Relationship (These characters had no pre-existing relationships.)
- Character (There was nothing terribly unique about anyone.)
- Dynamic (Nobody was particularly absurd.)

The Path chosen here was Premise. Lindsay thought she locked her keys in the car.

The Weapon of choice was Pattern. Every person who came across Lindsay had a tool that could help her except that it didn't exactly work out for her.

Using only one Path and one Weapon, we managed to create a delightful scene that utilized Walk-Ons and had a clear Edit point.

Improv Wins!

When we play Patterns, we allow ourselves the opportunity to flip the Pattern in the end, which is what happened when it wasn't Lindsay's car all along. We never see Lindsay's reaction to this, as the scene was edited as The Box was being opened.[2]

So at this point, the diligent improv student is thinking: "Isn't every person in the scene a Character?"

To varying degrees, yes.

"Doesn't everybody onstage have a Relationship?"

Okay, sure.

"How can there ever not be a Premise between these people, even if they are standing completely still and not saying a word?"

All right, we get it.[3]

---

[2] Find more on Patterns and Devices (tap-outs, walk-ons, etc.) in Chapter 8.

[3] As with almost every lesson in improv, these theories at times can also be shape-shifters.

In a great many scenes, following Paths & Weapons will make your improv maps amazing to explore.

But sometimes we do that one scene where everyone onstage pushes their chairs together and makes peeping noises the entire time, and for whatever magical reason, the audience went nuts, loved it, and remembers it forever.

Was the chair beeping scene The Perfect Scene?

Who knows?

It's all a matter of opinion.

OH GOSH, ONE MORE EXAMPLE TIME!

Yes, it's absolutely true that any two performers in the scene could have a Relationship, Premise, Character, Dynamic, Pattern, Setting, and Game simply based on the fact that they are onstage.

Even the two strangers (Relationship/Dynamic) wearing business suits (Character) at the bus stop (Setting) waiting for the bus (Premise) that never seems to come (Pattern), yet they don't give up (Game) contains all of these elements.

Until a Path is chosen and embraced, however, the scene is a certified snooze-fest.

By simply highlighting just one Path, the scene can jump in quality:

Two strangers (Relationship/Dynamic), one wearing a business suit (Character) and the other wearing a bathing suit (Character), at the bus stop (Setting), wait for the bus (Premise) that never seems to come (Pattern); yet they don't give up (Game).

Now there's something to talk about.

The business suit guy can ask, "Where are you going dressed like that?" and the bathing suit guy can reply, "Where are *you* going dressed like *that?*"

We've got ourselves an interesting character waiting for the bus and the entertained audience keeps their cellphones and Game Boys in their damn pockets.

Now let's combine the Path with a Weapon and watch the scene become magnetic:

Two strangers (Relationship/Dynamic), one wearing a business suit (Character) and the other wearing a bathing suit (Character), at the bus stop (Setting), waiting for the bus (Premise) that never seems to come (Pattern), and every minute that passes, the strangers count all of the things they could be doing instead of waiting for the bus (Game).

"I'm missing a very important meeting right now."

"I could be swimming right now."

"My bosses are going to be so mad at me."

"My friends are going to be disappointed that I didn't make it."

And a pattern emerges!

Both men are expressing their sadness, but neither are really talking to the other.

Imagine this scene going on for a few minutes as both men stare in the distance looking for the bus. The lack of eye contact becomes our "Box" and the longer we wait to Open the Box, the more life that our scene has.

"I should just take off this coat and tie and just go out and have fun today."

"I should just be patient and know that if it's meant to be, the bus will arrive."

Another performer jumps onstage, opens the bus door, and shouts, "Where to, boys?"

Then, for the first time all scene long, the business guy and bathing suit guy finally make eye contact.

We can anticipate what's next: Edit![4]

---

[4] **The Pleasant Paradox:** The point of the scene that looks, feels and smells like the edit, but the improvisers know that there is another line, gesture, or move remaining. In the description above, the edit could come as the business suit guy and bathing suit guy make eye contact.

We'd classify this last example as a Character/Game scene and most of our efforts should be centered on heightening these elements.

It's all we need. Moving past Character and Game could clutter and confuse.

But is nailing Character/Game/Setting more impressive than nailing Character/Game?

Not necessarily, especially since the right combination of Path and Weapon for you might organically create a Setting, so you can cross that off your scene to-do list.

Combining Paths is tricky.

Let's say there's a scene in which a group of gentlemen are confronted by a prostitute who uses traditional advertising methods for her business (she has flyers, a business card, radio commercials).

This is a Premise Path.

If other prostitutes Walk-On to the scene, really hammering home the point that *they are prostitutes* (they are loud, desperate, flirty – like normal prostitutes), then we're combining the Premise Path with a Character Path.

If the new prostitutes are taking focus away from the original (the Trunk), then we're not honoring the beginning of the scene.

Finding the right combination of Paths and Weapons will be unique for you and your group.

If you come from an acting background, you'll most likely embrace the Path of Character because you understand that the way you stand, sound, and move all feed into who you are onstage.

Those of us who are specifically pursuing a career in comedy most often target a Premise Path because we can easily wrap our minds around what is funny about a certain situation.

We're experiencing **The Pleasant Paradox** here because what if the edit doesn't come and both performers shout the words, "To the swimming pool!"
Then edit.
It's arguably even better than the initial edit point.
Either edit works and is funny, thus, **The Pleasant Paradox**!

If your particular life background has you on the lookout for a Relationship Path, then perhaps the Weapon is going to be where *your unique style* comes into play.

The Weapons we select are almost always a direct result of our training backgrounds and personal preferences.

CHAPTER 7

A Big Fat Path
Straight/Absurd Dynamic

This is the part where we talk about fused, arbitrary percentages.

These numbers are based on estimations and averages from 2003 onwards, culled from an amalgamation of classes taught in a number of different places as well as stage time gained at our home theaters and across the United States.

Because this test group is broader than just one training center, just one instructor (both Chris and Tami), or just one stage, we feel it's pretty much exactly what's up.

For real.

Between the two of us, we've logged over 3,000 hours of teaching, coaching, and directing improv. We have spent over 1,000 hours onstage performing and about 2,000 hours watching improv.

Pretty much all the other remaining time has been spent either talking about improv or what food we want to eat[1].

So, you see, that's exactly what's up for real, for real.

Okay.

Let's say in your first year of improv, you do 200 scenes. Out of those 200 scenes, it's safe to wager that at least 75% of those scenes had elements of the Straight/Absurd Dynamic.

But what if feeling "safe" isn't appealing to us? What if we're feeling wildly confident and bold? Let's double that wager and say the percentage is closer to 85%.

---

[1]Mainly pulled pork, sushi, pizza, or badass fresh juices. We'll come perform in your town in exchange for any of these.
We're talking to you, Kansas City.

Why so cocky?

Because we've seen it with our own eyes, a combined gazillion hours of eye-seeing!

Straight/Absurd

Improv organically breeds the Straight/Absurd Dynamic.

When we are trained to see it, before our very eyes, the scene boasts a crisp blueprint of character, game, premise, relationship, and setting - all the elements of Paths and Weapons neatly laid before us and ripe for the picking.

Some scenes beg to be played true straight/absurd from the first lines, some merely want to touch on aspects of it, and other scenes want to mingle straight/absurd with some other scene-driving element.

You decide the funniest choice and ride that lightning.

Most likely, as beginning improvisers, we don't know exactly what to do with that dynamic, so our scenes temper into a lukewarm porridge (rather than revving up to a hot rod wearing sunglasses scene!).

However, when we train our bodies and brains to recognize components of straight/absurd work, we can choose to harness or dismiss the dynamic, both to our and the scene's advantage.

But how do we recognize the Path of Straight/Absurd in our scenes?

Let's chill with an example first.

EXAMPLE TIME!

Mike Spara walks into a scene, sees that there is a box of pizza on the table, opens the box, and takes a slice from the box.

He then proceeds to sit and carefully chow down on the pizza.

Vanessa joins the scene, wild-eyed. She zips over to the pizza box, flips the lid open, snatches a slice, and shoves it into her mouth with a hysterical ferocity and nom-nom noises.

No one has said a word yet in this scene, yet already we have the trailhead coming into view. Recognizing the Facts[2] in the scene, Mike appears to be more of a straight character, Vanessa absurd.

---

[2] Facts are the indisputable elements of a scene that everyone in the scene can agree are true. We are definitely in the aquarium because we just talked about all the different kinds of fish in this aquarium tank.

Improv is full of confusing signals and we complicate things by not paying attention to The Facts. When we assume too much that's not based on Fact in a scene, we often end up discussing them with lines like, "I thought when you said _____, you wanted me to do _____," or, "I was thinking we were all in the spaceship so that's why I did the space stuff."

Experienced improvisers who have worked in a group for a while can usually pick up on each other's signals and move fluidly in a scene, trusting everyone is on the same page with a number of assumptions.

If it's important to you in this scene that we are in the spaceship, make it a fact. Show us that this is the spaceship. Say something like, "I can't get my turbo blaster to work, they just don't make space ships like they used to!"

Then everyone in the scene understands our Setting and they won't be lost when you start doing all that space stuff!

There is no such thing as being too clear with each other. When we have our facts nailed at the top of a scene, we can all move down our path together more confidently!

There are, of course, more clever ways than others to be clear. We exercise the mantra *Show Don't Tell*, and that helps a lot!

First, let's get some parameters to build from (choose a Weapon!).

What makes it the funniest possible scenario for her to be eating pizza like a crazy person?

If Mike offers the line, "This is some crazy party, huh," he has begun to explain away her behavior, making it less absurd.

However, if Mike offers the line, "Wakes like this are so sad," he is making her behavior potentially more absurd, since most people at a funeral wake would be somber and reserved.

It's the straight person's job to help make the absurd person more absurd, so probably "funeral wake" is a better choice than "crazy party" to demonstrate this dynamic.

We have our Weapon - the Setting of a wake. We can now apply our old trusty "If this is true, then what else is true" trick to the scene.

If Vanessa eats pizza like a maniac, then what else is true about Vanessa?

How about if we see what she does with something similar to pizza, like a drink!

Mike reacts to her gobbling up the pizza with a slightly puzzled look and then tries to engage her again. "Well, at least there's an open bar, huh?"

If Vanessa attacked the pizza, she'll probably react similarly to booze. Mike has set her up to either fill up a bunch of glasses to toss down her throat or gulp straight from the bottle or something that echoes her pizza attack.

Thanks, Mike!

We now have two beats of this dynamic laid out before us. For improv students familiar with straight/absurd work, the rest of this scene is cookie cake[3].

---

[3] The top-ranked treat to give a debuting improv troupe is cookie cake. The lowest-ranked is anything besides a cookie cake.

We don't know exactly what she'll do when it's time for the viewing of the body, but we can start gaining a pretty good idea. The invisible script is being written as the audience leans closer to the stage!

It's Mike's job for the remainder of this scene to help set Vanessa up to show the audience the catalogue of her character's absurdity. He does this by making realistic, rational offers to her.

As the straight character, Mike is the only one in the scene who speaks with any true authority. He's the "trustworthy" one, the one the audience will identify with logically. He speaks with the voice of the audience. He will help define the reality of this scene (like defining that this was indeed a wake) by making these offers.

If we know that she will inhale a slice a pizza and guzzle booze, then what else would also exist in this setting (a wake) that she could filter through her absurdity? We're laughing at Vanessa, but Mike is lobbing her softballs.

Mike and Vanessa get some dialogue going in the scene and we discover that Mike is only at the wake to support his co-worker whose Grandfather has passed away.

It would make the most absurd sense in this scene for Vanessa to be close to the deceased (wife, daughter, best friend).

Perhaps she is assigned to do the eulogy and wants to run it by Mike (but she doesn't do a traditional eulogy, she filters the eulogy through her character and perhaps it's a Top 5 List of All The Badass Hiding Places in Grandpa's House,[4] or a recipe for bringing Grandpa back to life, or a messy, lame limerick, etc.).

---

[4] 5. In the tub.

4. Under the sink.

3. Between the bookshelf and wall, next to the weird record player.

2. Aunt Laurie's armoire.

1. Directly behind Grandpa's back.

Mike can assess the Setting of "a wake" and gradually make offers based on this setting for Vanessa to heighten her character's absurdity and to heighten the absurdity of the scene.

What else exists at a wake? Other family members, flowers, mementos of the deceased - all of these Facts can be utilized to heighten Vanessa's character.

We know that if her eulogy is some crazy list of hiding places, then if we comment that all of the flowers in the room are beautiful, she can absolutely engage us in some diatribe about how she can never get the flowers to confess to what happened last summer at flower camp.

She can say all these nutso things because through our beats of this scene, she's in anything-goes-as-long-as-it's-hugging-her-absurd zone.

It is also Mike's job to heighten his side of this situation. If his reason for speaking to Vanessa in the first place is that he is emotionally fragile because his own mother is sick, then Vanessa seems even more terrible.

The more the straight person is a fully fleshed-out character, the more the absurd person's actions are attached to an impact.

The straight character is very much the invisible hand of the scene. He guides us along through the Beats and his reactions pace out the entire scene.

It's a bit of a bend in reality in some scenes, however, so it's important to note that the "improv-straight" reality might depart slightly from "real-straight" reality.

In the example above, it might be more realistic (if this scene were to take place in real life) that Mike would avoid any sort of confrontation altogether with Vanessa by not talking to her in the first place.

But that wouldn't make for a very good scene in improv.

So in improv, we suspend belief as far as we can while still allowing the straight character to exist in some level of engagement with the absurd character, in order to propel the scene forward.

Once the straight and absurd characters become engaged, the straight character lengthens and draws out the Beats of the scene by employing his Emotion Wheel of responses to the absurd character.

It's tricky, though, because it's also tempting to start to closely identify and share perspective with the absurd person, but that makes you become absurd yourself![5]

It's easy to jump the gun as the straight person and get trapped in a very uncomfortable scene with a crazy person.

That's why the Emotion Wheel is so important.

---

[5] Straight person, beware! Do not get on board with the absurdity! Sometimes it feels like a safer/easier choice to get wacky and start gobbling pizza, but usually it just translates as insecurity (not playfulness) to the audience.

It's really easy to let the scene slip from your grip by engaging the absurdity too much.

We don't want to deny the absurdity outright, we want to nurse it, lead it on, and build it up to the big strong absurd beast it wants to be!

The Emotion Wheel!

When Vanessa gulps down half a bottle of Irish whiskey, the straight character might want to flip out, call out how absurd she is, and leave the room. But in order to maintain the scene, he needs to patiently deal with each absurd offer.

Column A Absurd Offer	Column B Straight Reaction
• Vanessa gobbles up pizza. • Vanessa guzzles whiskey. • Vanessa yells at the flowers. • Vanessa paraphrases eulogy. • Vanessa flirts with family members.	• Mike looks at her puzzled. • Mike is curious. • Mike is disbelieving. • Mike is confused. • Mike nervously laughs.

These are all straight reactions to these actions, but they are specific and paired down from the biggest get-the-heck-outta-here knee-jerk reactions.

With each choice he makes by engaging his Emotion Wheel, he is giving more life to the scene, building tension, and helping to heighten the scene.

If Mike jumps from curious to disbelieving to get-the-heck-outta-here, we have lost all the sweet opportunities for Vanessa to tell us about her eulogy, show us her Grandpa tattoo, etc.

For all of these reasons (invisible hand, trustworthy character, Emotion Wheel, feeding offers to the absurd person), being the straight person in an improv scene is a difficult job.

And many beginning improvisers feel like it's the less fun role to play.

Yes, the absurd person gets most of the laughs a lot of the time, especially for new improvisers. But the more adept we become at playing straight, the more we learn to garner laughs for ourselves through strong offers, playing the Emotion Wheel intelligently and with smart timing.

Let's explore this further with another example!

EXAMPLE TIME AGAIN!

Michael Foulk and Amy Jordan are decorating their Christmas tree together for the first time since they got married.

Michael puts an ornament on the tree and tells a sweet story about how his grandmother made it when she was a little girl growing up in Germany.

Amy then grabs one of her ornaments, a shrunken head. She tells a sweet story about how it was the head of her great grandfather who got caught cheating on her great grandmother and so she shrunk his head.

Michael, rather than going to his Emotion Wheel and responding with, let's say, *curious disbelief*, replies to Amy's ornament with, "So, your people are head-shrinkers? You didn't tell me that before we got married. What's next, you're also a cannibal?"

By calling out her first offer of absurdity, Michael has started to reroute the scene from a perfectly delightful straight/absurd (and possibly richly-patterned) game of Terrible First Christmas (where we actually get to *see* Amy be a cannibal) to Couple Arguing About Stuff scene.

Show us, don't tell us!

Show us that she comes from a long line of head-shrinkers (the ornament), who feast on humans (the Christmas "goose" is the neighbor boy), who chant blood-curdling hymns to the Dark Lord (creepy Christmas carols), and at midnight is gifted with the power of shape-shifting by a mad shaman bathed in lamb's blood (Santa!).

SHOW.

DON'T TELL.

EXERCISE: ABSURDITY EXPLOSION!

Some improvisers slip right into absurdity like a hand in a glove. It's what they joined improv to do. They can't wait to show off their crazy Uncle Paulie character!

That's awesome. Fly high, brave birdies!

But others have a more difficult time accessing absurdity, which is fine, too.

For those students, we like to run an exercise that helps get them comfortable with leaving the logic behind.

In this exercise, we assign one student to play the straight character - it's their job to make real, logical offers to the absurd person.

After each line from the straight person, the absurd person takes one word from that line and repeats it, using it to inspire their next line and direction of absurdity.

Straight Person: It's always difficult to come back to **work** after a holiday, huh?

Absurd Person: You call this **work**? When I'm at home on the weekends, that's work to me!

Straight Person: Not me, I feel like every hour I'm here is like a day...it's not even **lunch** yet.

Absurd Person: At my house, I *am* **lunch**. Yeah, I have to hide myself in the tub so my wife and kids don't hunt and devour me!

Straight Person: Sure, I know what you mean. Families can take a **toll** on you...

Absurd Person: I paid the **toll**! My wife assumes the form of a troll in our foyer and demands shiny gold pieces from me, which she says will ensure my safe passage, but somehow the Toll Troll always gets me...

By taking one word from the straight character's line, the absurd character has begun to form a character that's unique to that specific scene - the guy who literally believes that his life is in danger when he is at home among his family.

This exercise forces not only the absurd character to listen to each offer being made by the straight character, but it also forces the straight character to help *be more listenable*[6] as well as set up the absurd character.

It is the job of both straight and absurd characters to heighten the game of the scene. When we recognize that we are both moving the scene forward, we become more thoughtful about our straight offers and absurd responses, building tighter, more aligned scene work.

---

[6] Be perceptive! Make the most clear and intelligent and fun-for-both-of-us offers into the scene. When we see improvisers trying to trick each other or trip up their scene partners for a quick laugh, it feels like the opposite of what we are supposed to be doing - make each other look like rock stars!

Important Note on Dynamic Characters!

Just because you are playing straight doesn't mean you can't play that really sweet wizard character you've been working on!

Character doesn't define dynamic. Perspective defines dynamic.

You can absolutely play the Wizard from the Three Forest Moons, but speak to the scene with a rational, "voice of the audience" perspective.

Even if the character who is playing absurd in the scene is just some guy (not a wizard), that guy could be coming from the perspective of: *Everything is awesome, and by the way, I'm totally on a killing spree, but I make it look like an accident, oops!*

Another Important Note on Dynamic Characters!

If you are playing a child,[7] you are not automatically absurd.

Children are absurd in nature.

Just like drunks. Or junkies.

If a child/drunk/junkie is acting like a child/drunk/junkie, then they are being true to their character and therefore being "straight."

If the child/drunk/junkie is acting like a super-eloquent 19th century senator from South Carolina, then he is being absurd.

---

[7] **Playing children:**
Sometimes making the choice to play a child is just downright difficult for an audience to watch and/or it's irritating for your scene partner to play with.
Play characters that are likable to some degree.
Many times, a child character is annoying, demanding, screechy, unreasonable, and ultimately stalls a scene because they refuse to give in on their, "I want!"
A likable child, the child that is childlike in every way, but happens to give Mommy really great advice, is a much more playful choice.
The same with drunks and junkies - they have to have some degree of likability.

Absurd-Absurd in a Straight Setting

Sarah and Patrick both run onstage, open car doors, and quickly belt themselves in, locking the doors.

They mirror each other's energy, communicating that they are freaked out about being in the outside world, and it is quickly revealed that the outside world they are talking about is a very ordinary and normal world.

Through their conversation, we learn that their car is parked in a driveway, on a street in a normal neighborhood.

Nothing is absurd about the environment.

They are the absurd element.

So how do we play two absurd characters in a scene? Balance it with the setting!

When both absurd characters in the scene understand that the duty of their setting is to provide them with setups through which they can filter their absurdity, the dynamic applies just as it does in the explanations above.

Characters that rarely earn the favor of the audience: annoying children, stupid valley girls, unfunny racist hicks (see "Racism" below), and the unintelligible bear that tries to eat everyone in the scene.

Racism:

Funny, smart, fake-racism is awesome. Unfunny, stupid, seemingly too-real racism blows.

We encourage everyone to experiment with edgy comedy. We like to push boundaries and challenge conventions.

Absolutely play Hitler, show us your gun-loving Klansman, be a crazed Cambodian despot - but be smart about it.

Make sure, though, that in addition to saying all the terrible things that you're saying as that character that you are also communicating to the audience: "I am making this choice because I know it is a terrible thing and I am taking all power out of these words by making it ridiculous."

NOT: "Look, I'm playing the racist stereotype of a black man! It's funny because I'm black!"

Simply playing a stereotype is not a joke...it's just a lame one-note caricature.

The setting becomes the straight element. All of the things that are true and real in a car will now serve as offers from the straight component.

If the characters they've established are frightened of all the things that exist in their very normal world, what happens when Sarah tries to start the car? ("OMG why is it growling at us!?!")

What about when they have to look at a map? ("This is just a picture of LINES!!!")

How about that reflection in the rear view mirror? (WHO IS THAT GUY WHO LOOKS LIKE ME WHO'S LOOKING AT ME!?!)

Straight-Straight in an Absurd Setting

On the other side of this, when we have two straight characters in an absurd setting, the setting is acting as the nutso wackadoo aspect of the scene.

Clay and Christie are discussing detailed plans for their anniversary. Through their actions, dialogue, and object work onstage, we can see that they are boarding themselves up in their house against some terrible monster attack.

Clay is loading a gigantic gun, Christie is praying to a shrine, Clay is fortifying a door with chairs and tables, Christie is making Molotov cocktails.

The setting can speak to us via cast members on the sidelines, a radio announcer telling us that the monster is within the city limits, a huge crash, or screams from outside, etc.[8]

---

[8] One radio announcer is enough.

Yes, Christie and Clay are being somewhat absurd by not totally freaking out about the monsters. But we feel that the stronger choice is not spinning the scene towards dealing with the monster attack, but developing an interesting dynamic to balance against the monster attack.

We have to suspend a little belief to allow this scene to have legs.

These kinds of scenes are less common, but when they do emerge, it's fun to apply the Straight/Absurd Dynamic approach to the scene in addition to following other scene-driving elements.

CHAPTER 8

If There's a Cake in the Living Room, There's a Brownie in the Basement

Discovering and Using Patterns in Scene Work and Devices

Derek and Kelly are on a date at the movies. They are holding hands and making eye contact. This date is going pretty well.

Derek leans over to Kelly and says, "The monster is going to explode when the little girl pours water on him and then-"

Kelly stops Derek mid-sentence and asks, "Did you already see this movie?"

He answers, "Yes," as if it were obvious.

For a moment, Kelly's face shows vague disappointment, but then she makes an unconventional response choice - Kelly's character gets turned on by the revelation that Derek's character has already seen the movie.

The pairing of the absurd premise (going on a date to see a movie you've already seen) with the unconventional/weird response (being turned on by your date not doing anything special) is a bright neon flag in a scene.

That is something!

The scene at this point is not about dynamics. Neither character has been established as strictly straight or absurd, and they are of the same status.

It's also not a strong character or relationship scene: both characters are pretty plain, aside from their one strange quirk, and these characters have not been named, nor is their relationship 100% specific (First date? Married? Best Date Ever?[1]).

Therefore, the path for this scene is the coupling of two strange things: the man who has "been there, done that" already on his date and the woman who is aroused by this rendezvous being nothing special to her date.

This pattern repeats when Kelly offers him some of her popcorn and he admits to not only having already eaten, but he specifically had popcorn earlier today.
This, of course, turns Kelly on even more.
He had popcorn already! Swoon swoon!

Our flag is flapping in the breeze now. All other paths are cut off, and we have to keep heightening the two things we know in this scene, because they're all that matters now.

They've played this Pattern so hard that it feels like there's a hundred ways for this scene to go, yet they want to pick the best choice - the choice that most reflects Derek's strange decision to take Kelly to a movie he's already seen, on a day when he already ate popcorn, and her tendency to get turned on by his prior experiences.

When an usher walks onto the scene and tells Derek that, since his ticket is only good for one matinee movie,

---

[1] Worst Footnote Ever: Next time you find yourself about to claim something is the "best (or worst) ___ ever," try and replace those words with something you would actually say in that situation.

For example, if you're on the worst date ever, you might find yourself saying something like, "Wow, you're really doing that," in a sarcastic tone when responding to your date soaking up his soup with his necktie.

he has to leave the theater immediately, and we realize that he's been there all day with one movie ticket on presumably several different dates!

So of course this date that he's on is no big deal!

This final revelation causes Kelly to have a huge orgasm.

Edit.

It's a successful scene because of the Pattern work. Not only did Derek already eat, but he already specifically ate *popcorn*. This heightens the fact that he's already seen this same exact movie.

Since we're playing the Patterns, he's not only done these things with a different girl, *but he did them all today.*

If in our third beat, we don't learn that Derek has been on multiple dates in the same theater watching the same movie and eating the same popcorn (in presumably the same seat) **on the same day,** it's less funny.

Making the scene occur on the same day increases the absurdity of the entire situation, and if we honor the Pattern, we'll achieve this every time.

Playing the Patterns is the fastest way to make your improv look like sketch comedy. The more detail and care you put into each line or gesture, the more you "write" your scene.

Sticking to the example above, if after the second move (popcorn), any device is used to do anything other than show how Derek has already done these things *today*, then the scene drops in quality.

Discovering and heightening patterns isn't easy.

In classes at The New Movement, we introduce these concepts in Level 3 and we spend a significant amount of time on them. The more analytical brains might pick up on them easier than the more fluid thinkers.

Chances are, you're already familiar with the exercise below, but we encourage you to follow along with our tweaks so you can more closely identify with the types of patterns we're discussing.

THE ULTIMATE PATTERN EXERCISE

The performers all stand in a circle.

One person initiates the pattern by pointing at someone and saying a word or phrase.

Let's say it's, "Blue."

That person then points to someone else and says what they feel will solidify the pattern.

Let's say they choose, "Red."

When the third person points and says, "Green," it's abundantly clear that our pattern is "Colors," so the players continue to point and say a color until the last person points back at the first.

Then on the count of three, they all say what the pattern is.

If everyone responds with "Colors," then congratulations, you've nailed the Pattern. Granted, it's probably the easiest Pattern of all,[2] but you've nailed it.

High-fives!

Now let's explore an alternative route.

If the second person receives the initiation, "Blue," and responds with, "Sky," the pattern of "Colors" is off the board because "Sky" is not a color.

So our third person is put in a difficult position here. If she says, "Red," perhaps the next person says, "Blood," thus creating a slightly more complex, but still follow-able A-B, A-B, A-B pattern.

Blue/Sky!

Red/Blood!

Yellow/Banana!

High-fives!!

---

[2] See also: "Numbers" and "Fast-Food Hamburger Joints."

But what about this?

If our third person says, "Cloud," what will the next person say?

Perhaps "Rain" or "Bird" or "Plane."

This is a vague road to travel down. What will these people say on the count of three?

"Things found in the sky?"

The scene equivalent here is a "Listing Scene," which may not be as fun.

High-five?

And what if this happens?

If the second person receives the word "Blue" and responds with, "Water," and then we get to "Boat" and then "Vacation" and then "Beach" and then "Sand," what exactly are we talking about?

On the count of three, these participants will have no idea what to respond with, "Things...Places...A Vacation...where there is water involved....?"

They've succumbed to Word Association, the arch nemesis of Pattern.

~~High-five.~~

Word Association

True story: Once upon a time, Chris was in a delightful scene where he was playing the boyfriend and was clearly working up the nerve to propose to his girlfriend.

It was indicated that they weren't at a fancy restaurant and his character was apologetic for not being well-equipped financially.

When the waiter appeared and asked how the baby back ribs were, they responded positively and moved on with the scene.

Suddenly, a pair of improvisers jumped onstage and began signing the baby back ribs jingle from the famous old Chili's commercial.

Barf.

Since then, we've labeled moments like this one as Word Association. The improviser hears something that makes him think of something and he's gotta come out and say it.

See also when a scene just so happens to be on a film set and improvisers rush to become the camera crew and then feel the need to justify their presence (often wondering aloud if their boom mic is in the shot).

It's a habit more commonly found in improv babies and teens. It's like dropping a bomb in the middle of your Relationship, leaving the performers to scramble and pick up the pieces.

If the edit doesn't come right then, then maybe you're stuck feeling the need to justify the presence of the baby back ribs jingle.

If the edit does come right away, then your patient two-person Relationship-based scene just ended on the baby back ribs jingle.

When Word Association shows up, everyone loses.

To be fair, playing Patterns is a delightful way to pull yourself out of a complicated situation like the example above.

If we're able to maintain the relationship while also playing the Pattern of "commercial jingles being sung while you're trying to have a romantic moment," then bravo!

Let's say we continue this scene by creating a Pattern with romantic moments and jingles.

The baby back ribs guys pop off the stage and we continue on with our date.

Chris raises his glass and starts to sweetly propose a toast to his girlfriend.

The waiter returns and asks if they're enjoying the wine.

The man responds with, "I'm loving it!"

Cue the two jingle singers. They jump onstage and sing the McDonald's commercial jingle, "Ba-da-ba-ba-ba....I'm lovin' it!"

The second beat of the jingle Pattern is obtained and has now solidified that the waiter introduces the opportunity for the jingle singers.

When the waiter returns the third time with a dessert menu and casually asks if the couple lives in the neighborhood, the man in the scene replies that they do, and thus our jingle singers are set up to belt out the well-known Applebee's restaurant jingle, "Eatin' Good in the Neighborhood."

It's significantly more difficult to pull this off and it's the opposite of grounded, but some people like to introduce challenges and enjoy pop-culture references.

Be aware, though, that one appearance of the commercial jingle equals Word Association.

Multiple appearances equals Pattern work.

In either case, it's not what the Trunk of the scene was about (it was about a low-budget marriage proposal), so we've already lost The Perfect Scene.

We're often told that we have to focus on "Listening" to become successful improvisers.

Why not spend some time making yourself more "Listenable"?[3] Staying in the moment of the scene will help us detach from the temptation of Word Association, and everything that comes out of our mouths will instantly weigh more.

---

[3] Making yourself more Listenable: From the beginning of the scene, talk about things happening NOW in the scene between US.

When we make ourselves relatable, personal, and attached to the scene, it's so much easier for our partner to play with us.

MUTHA-FUCKIN' EXAMPLE TIME!

Let's make sure we've got this. Here's a list of right and wrong Patterns, complete with scene translations and difficulty levels.

Example #1:
Louisiana-Florida-Montana-California-Maryland
PATTERN: States.
DIFFICULTY LEVEL: Easy
SCENE TRANSLATION: Doctor reveals that his patient is going to die.

Example #2:
Louisiana-Mississippi-Alabama-Florida-Georgia
PATTERN: States that border each other.
DIFFICULTY LEVEL: Medium
SCENE TRANSLATION: Doctor reveals that his patient is going to die via an X-ray slide show.

Example #3:
Louisiana-Lakes-Latitude-Longitude-Land
PATTERN: Things on a map that begin with L
DIFFICULTY LEVEL: Hard
SCENE TRANSLATION: Doctor reveals that his patient is going to die via an X-ray slide show. Each X-ray shown causes the patient to bring up a specific memory involving each body part on the X-ray that slowly explains the cause of death.

Example #4:
Louisiana-State-Capital-D.C.-Alphabet
PATTERN: Nothing
DIFFICULTY LEVEL: N/A
SCENE TRANSLATION: Together, these words don't mean anything. We say "state" because that's what "Louisiana" is and we say "Alphabet" because "D.C." are letters of the alphabet. It means nothing, and therefore, this scene will likely mean nothing.

Note how all four of the above examples use the same initiation. It's what we do with this that makes our scene unique.

The opening line of, "Louisiana," could mean a million things. When the reply is, "Mississippi," there is a very strong suggestion that this scene is going to be about "Bordering States."

If our third line is, "Oregon," our scene is still about "States," though it lacks the hyper-specificity and quality of "Bordering States."

Here's another set of examples highlighting how vastly different our scene can become based on the second line of dialogue.

Example #5:
American Eagle-Gap-Banana Republic-Hollister-JC Penney
PATTERN: Clothing stores
DIFFICULTY LEVEL: Medium

Example #6:
American Eagle-George Washington-Red, White, and Blue-Apple Pie-Freedom
PATTERN: American shit
DIFFICULTY LEVEL: Medium

Example #7:
American Eagle-Canadian Bacon-Chinese Medicine-French Bread-Italian Cream Soda
PATTERN: Country/Noun
DIFFICULTY LEVEL: Medium

While all the initiating lines are the same, the response dictates the rest of the scene.

It requires intense listening throughout.

MORE EXAMPLES, PLEASE!

American Eagle-Canadian Bacon-Chinese Medicine-Gap-Freedom

Here we have a lack of listening bringing down an otherwise fine scene.

Whoever says, "Gap," is playing off the initiation of "American Eagle" when we've clearly chosen the route of Country/Noun instead of Clothing Stores.

This often hurts us when we are spending time on the sidelines thinking of a reason to Walk On or Tap In on a scene and we aren't paying attention to the action.

"Gap" was spending too much time in his own head and not enough time collaborating and listening.

Milk-Ice Cream-Sugar-Cocaine-Whipped Cream

We have a jokester on our hands here. Yes, *Cocaine* is a white substance that people consume, but it's clearly not in the same family because cocaine isn't found in most kitchens.

We have a decision to make. Is our pattern "anything white" or is it "white substance that people often consume"?

If it's "anything white," it loses credibility because there are many things that are white - clouds, cotton, snow.

Our scene is more interesting if we stick to "white substance that people often consume" because it is more specific.

However...

Milk-Ice Cream-Sugar-Whipped Cream-Cocaine

This pattern brings up an interesting debate.

Once the pattern is set, can we have a little fun with it at the end? Can we bend it, shape it, tease it?

Absolutely! Yes we can!

This pattern is especially interesting because *Cocaine* remains a "white substance that people consume."[4]

The improviser is broadening the scope of the pattern towards the end of the pattern, but keeping it in the family.

Milk-Ice Cream-Sugar-Whipped Cream-Unicorn works as well, but it breaks really far away from the pattern, so we have to ask ourselves, is *Unicorn* funnier than *Cocaine*?[5]

In this case, we strongly believe that it is not. Anyone in the theater can pick up on "anything white," but it takes a Pattern-seeking improviser to quickly pick up "white substance that people consume," and then have the skill to bend the pattern to include *Cocaine*.

And when *Cocaine* appears, the Box is Opened.

---

[4] In some parts of the world, we can insert the word "often" at the end of this phrase! Zing zap zop!

[5] Unless the Unicorn is riding another Unicorn, then absolutely not.

JUST *ONE MORE* EXAMPLE TIME!

Applying the above mode of thought to scenes is easier than you may think. If we treat each line from the very beginning like it's a precious piece of our Pattern, we can do it!

> **GRACE: I'm quitting college and I'm becoming a clown.**
> **MOM: That's understandable. I'm very proud of you. We all are.**

Notice how with each piece of dialogue we eliminate more and more options. We are shrinking our world, making it much easier to navigate.

Grace's next move is crucial.

> **GRACE: I sold all the jewelry that you and Grandma gave me to attend clown academy.**
> **MOM: Honey, you've got to do whatever it takes to achieve your dream.**

Our scene is now dipped in concrete!

It's not debatable that we are dealing with a daughter who is taking an unconventional route to achieve her goals and a Mom who is going to see the positive side of any situation.

But we're not finished yet!

Our next move likely dictates the Path of this scene. Is the Mom going to be positive no matter what?

That's a Character Path and will likely include Tap Outs, like her Husband cancelling dinner to play pool with his friends.

She, of course, understands why he would do that.

Or is this about Grace not being able to get a rise out of anyone?

That's another Character Path that will likely include Tap Outs, like her friend initiating with, "Someone ate all of my leftovers."

Grace then admits that she did it, and then her friend is all, "You're probably hungrier than I am, so it's cool."

Since both characters are so strong, maybe this is a Premise scene. With a Premise, we can usually initiate a Split Scene and duplicate the Game, especially if the original Premise appears to be short-lived.

Patterns also enhance the quality of our group scene work. These work best when everyone onstage has something to do, *i.e.* every time Megan announces that someone broke something in the kitchen, Jenna scratches her head, Andy rubs his elbow, and Henry stretches his hamstrings.

All three people "doing anything to distract them" is significantly less funny than all three people "distracting themselves by tending to parts of their bodies."

ILLUSTRATION: HOW MANY THINGS CAN THIS SCENE BE ABOUT?

Two people step onstage. The scene can be about an infinite number of things.

Initiation Line: "You spilled paint on my sock, Tim!"

Now the scene can only be about 250 things.

Second Line: "I also crashed your car."

Now the scene can only be about 75 things.

Third Line: "This sock is important to me!"

We got it! This scene is about one thing – the damn sock!

Devices

Devices are like spices - it's fun to mix them into your meal, but you shouldn't shovel spoonfuls of them into your mouth.

There's nothing wrong with devices appearing in all of your scenes.

The trick is sprinkling the right amount at the right time.

Most devices will be used when the Trunk scene hits the ceiling.

In the previous example with Grace and Mom, it only took four lines to establish all the necessary details.

One way to heighten is to show that Mom (or Grace) is like this in <u>every</u> situation, and that requires the use of devices.

The Walk-On

The "salt" of devices! Commonly used, but too much gives your show a heart attack.

Most often paired with "Premise" or "Game" scenes.

The trick to most Walk-Ons is walking off and leaving the focus on the original scene.

Walk-Ons don't need to linger, and if you're not careful, you can be a loud and squeaky third wheel. Leaving the scene gives the performers an opportunity to deal with the information you've presented to them.

In the earlier example of Derek and Kelly, we used a Walk-On to heighten the premise of "Girl gets turned on the more Guy treats her less special."

The Walk-On wasn't crucial to the success of the scene, but it provided a nice clean finish. It's especially impressive to the audience to see the people on the sidelines as tuned into the scene as the people onstage.[6]

The Tap-Out

Most often paired with "Character" scenes.

When Stuart the Timid Whispering Teenager screws up his valedictorian speech because nobody could hear him, it makes sense that in our next scene, we see him as Stuart the Timid Whispering Adult and he's performing a high stress life-or-death surgery.

---

[6] **True Stories with Christopher Michael:** The funniest Walk On I've seen in real life came when I was working at a restaurant in Baton Rouge, coincidentally named Walk-Ons. My friend Truston called ahead to order a Cookie Bowl dessert to go. When he walked into the restaurant and gave the hostess his name, they gave him his order, not realizing he wanted it to go. He walked out and kept the bowl and spoons.

When a character becomes bigger than the scene, it's important to surround him with a new situation so that we can heighten the character.

A Tap-Out wouldn't be as effective in the earlier example of Derek and Kelly because neither character was bigger than the other. The words coming out of Derek's mouth matched up nicely with Kelly's setup and reactions. We can heighten within this Premise without removing one of the characters.

In the example with Grace and Mom, a "ceiling" was hit early, and turning this into a series of Tap-Outs helped us execute The Perfect Scene.

It's funny when Mom gives Grace the benefit of the doubt.

It's funnier when Mom gives Everyone the benefit of the doubt.

It's funniest when Mom gives Satan the benefit of the doubt, and BAM, the Box Has Been Opened.

Split Scenes

In the earlier example of Derek and Kelly at the movies, we can extend the life of this scene by splitting it.

In Split Scenes, we duplicate the established premise by bringing on another pair of improvisers into the same physical space, but usually a different location.

It becomes risky to maneuver both scenes in the same world but separate locations, but the benefits of nailing this are huge!

It's not unlike splitting a hand in Blackjack, so we asked our pal Kyle Austin (staff member at the Dallas Comedy House and expert gambler) to compare the two.

Kyle Austin: "_Splitting a hand in Blackjack is quite thrilling, as it doubles your responsibility as well as your chance to win (or lose)._
Playing both hands requires you to pay extra attention to what is going on around you (the other hands) while making the right moves for the two hands you just inherited. Because of the nature of splitting a hand, it's either a huge success or huge failure, though.

The thrill of splitting a blackjack hand and splitting an improv scene are very similar. Just remember not to be an adrenaline junkie and try to do it every time the opportunity "might be there."
Realistically, you don't want to split every Blackjack hand you can, and the same goes for improv.
Study your craft, make an educated decision, don't be scared, and let the process take over."

Derek and Kelly are on a date at the movies. They are holding hands and making eye contact.

When Derek lets Kelly in on what's about to happen on the screen, she stops him mid-sentence and asks if he's already seen this film.

He says yes and Kelly's face goes from being disappointed to being turned on.

This pattern repeats when Kelly offers him some of her popcorn, and he admits to not only having already ate, but he specifically had popcorn earlier today.

This, of course, turns Kelly on even more.

Another pair of performers enters the stage and quickly define their own setting, indicating they are splitting the scene, not joining it.

Denise asks Shaun if he wants to go to Maui on their honeymoon.

Sean stops her mid-sentence because that's where he went with his first wife.

At this point, anyone who is listening (including our audience) can figure out the Pattern.

Something interesting happens here though, as most audiences gladly come along for the ride, even though they can (arguably) predict what will happen next.

The boy in the scene will reveal that he already experienced whatever he is doing with a different girl and the girl he is presently with will get turned on.

For an audience, there is some very real joy in discovering what *these* people will do in this scene.

What will happen next?

They understand that Girl suggests X and guy's already done X and then girl will react pleasantly, but what will X be this time?

Add to this our first scene and we've got four people onstage seamlessly interacting with one another, reciting an invisible script, and what we've created is not only funny, but in many ways, magical.

Remember this: The Pattern is more specific than the Game, but not all games have a Pattern.

Pattern With Yourself

Many of the people who excel at Patterns often implement them within their own actions, adding extra elements to the scene to make it richer, meatier, juicier!

To the examples!

A librarian is getting hit on by a customer. He has a book open, and each time the flirtatious girl compliments him, he nervously turns a page.

When the girl touches him, he gets a bigger book.

When she finally propositions him, he pulls down the largest book on the shelf.

This scene is about the relationship between these two people, but the librarian has added an extra layer. He's communicating through the books and planting his own seeds. If he's able to accomplish this while also maintaining the relationship, then we've got an extra fun scene!

Now throughout the course of the show, turning pages in a book equals nervously receiving compliments. And for those really paying attention, book equals penis!

Imagine at the end of the show (let's say, 20 minutes from the library scene) when Housewife #1 asks Housewife #2 if she can borrow a book.

When Housewife #2 is impressed with the sexual explorations of Housewife #1, the audience realizes that book *still* equals penis.

A party host welcomes in the first guest who has brought a gift. The host places the gift on the counter.

A few beats later, another guest comes in with another gift. The host places this gift on top of the previous gift or throws away the first gift and replaces it with the new one or opens the two gifts and discovers they are compatible (batteries and a toy car!).

Imagine all of this in addition to whatever relationship or game is already in play between the characters!

A few beats later, a third guest can arrive with a third gift and the fun continues.

Bonus points for nobody referencing the gifts.

Spoiling the Bunch

You slept in the socks, walked around the house in those socks, played basketball in those socks, and then watched television in those same damn socks.

At the end of the night, you throw them in the laundry pile.

The next morning, a yucky stench rises from the pile.

You've just spoiled the bunch.

Every device used is a candidate to spoil the bunch.

There are lots of folks in the great big improv world who are anti-Tap-Out, who despise the Walk-On, and who say mean things about the Split Scene.

These people have seen one too many pairs of nasty socks in the laundry basket and they're over it.

No socks allowed.

Socks, however, are incredibly useful. They prevent blisters and keep you warm. You can slide across smooth surfaces. You can put them on your hand and make puppets.

Devices are also incredibly useful. They prevent complacency and keep scenes interesting. You can slide in and out of scenes and create smooth transitions. You can put them on your hand and make puppets.[7]

Since Walk-Ons don't require more than someone walking onstage and saying something, you will experience these the most.

When an inexperienced performer hears two people onstage discussing someone that isn't there, they often feel the need to fill in the blank (spoiling the bunch). Especially if the two people onstage are having a really good time doing a really good scene.

When Mommy and Daddy are arguing about who's going to feed the baby, the more you talk about the baby, the more someone is likely to take the bait and enter the scene as the baby.

Make yourself more "Listenable" by not focusing on the baby, but rather a series of things in the center of Mommy and Daddy's argument.

Tap-Outs are slightly more complex because they require direction and a little bit of mind reading. Being clear as to who you want to remain in the scene and who you want to leave will decrease how often you spoil the bunch.

When *being Tapped Out*, we recommend that you take the shortest route off the stage, as long as it's not through another person.

When *Tapping Out* someone else, we recommend that you indicate which direction you want the person to move.

---

[7] **Our friend and fellow TNM staff member Patrick Knisely on puppets:** "Improvising with puppets can improve one's more traditional improv skills. The dual focus on puppeteering and improvising can cause one to freeze up and lose focus on the puppeteering or the improvising; or with time and practice, it can free you up to be more in the moment.

When puppeteering, one goal is to have the audience's focus directed to the puppet. Learning how to direct that focus and breathe life into a puppet can help in those scenes where your hands are a bird or bat, or you're voicing a spirit offstage. The greatest benefit, however, is that of character work, especially absurd character work. Puppets are characters, and for those people who have a hard time improvising as characters, using a puppet can help train them to let go of their usual behavior and voice and become someone else."

Split Scenes are often spoiled by someone not realizing that the performers are probably in multiple locations.

This is sad because not listening is a very sad problem.

If two people walk onstage and don't make eye contact with you and they initiate a scene that is similar to yours, they are probably splitting it and don't need to be talked to.

If you're mad because they've heightened your scene, then go ahead and spoil the bunch by calling them out on it.

But then stay up all night because you feel so bad about it.

ILLUSTRATION: HOW TO PROPERLY PERFORM A TAP-OUT

SCENARIO 1

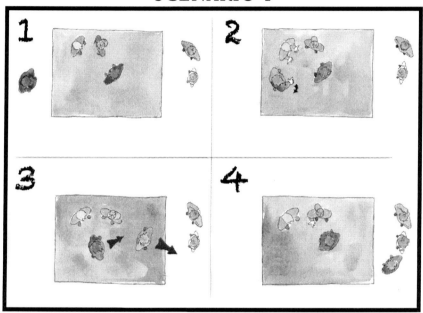

SCENARIO 2

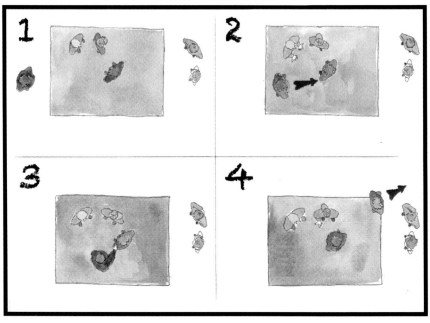

SCENARIO 3

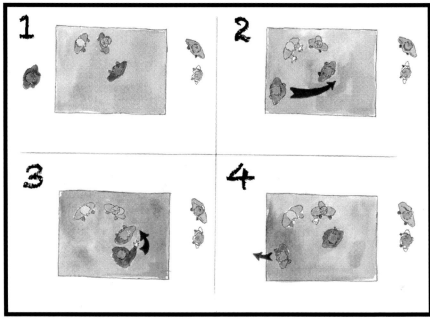

Breaking the Pattern

We welcome you to break the pattern once you feel you've hit the ceiling of your scene.

This can feel like a nice reward for all of your awesome work. It's also a pretty neat way to keep your group on the same page with edits. Because when everyone on the side comes out to edit the scene at the same time, something wonderful probably just happened.

In Conclusion

Playing the Pattern isn't for everyone.

Some people would rather play Twister than Chess, since Chess requires the performer to be borderline mathematical with their moves, which takes away the fun for a lot of folks.

To you Twister-loving people we say: No problem!

If you're feeling the Patterns, but the people you play with aren't on the same page, then play them with yourself.

We beg all of you, however, to always consider that if Grandpa is in an uproar because he cannot remember where he left his cake, and we discover it's in the living room, then Grandma's brownie is most definitely in the basement[8].

---

[8] And Aunt Laurie's cookie is in the bathroom, Cousin Evan's éclair is in the hallway, Brother Jason's milkshake is in the attic, and Baby Jack's candy is in the office.

PUT YOUR PATTERN TO THE QUIZ!

There are six people sitting in a circle. Person 1 initiates an Addicted-to-Disney-World Support Group scene. Persons 2, 3, and 4 join in clockwise fashion, adding why they are also addicted.

What does Person 5 and 6 do?

A) **Add why they are addicted to Disney World.**

B) **Person 6 says why he is addicted, then Person 5 breaks the pattern.**

C) **Person 5 says why she is addicted, then Person 6 breaks the pattern.**

D) **Donald Duck does a Walk-On.**

Option "**C**" is correct!

Since we're moving through the performers clockwise, we should keep this pattern alive. It's minor, but sweating the small stuff is huge.

Person 6 is the last person in the scene, so she has the right to break the pattern.

But how does she break the pattern?

    A) By admitting that she is also addicted to Disney World.

    B) By asking Person 5 more questions about their addiction.

    C) By singing *Circle of Life.*

    D) By admitting that she went to Disney World once as a kid and she'd like to go back.

Option "**D**" is the favorite here because she is delightfully breaking the pattern by not admitting to an addiction problem, rather that she's only been to Disney World once before and she'd like to go back.

This would turn the rest of the people against her, giving us plenty to play with for the rest of the scene.

After Person 6 breaks the pattern, what does Person 1 do?

    A) Call attention to the fact that Person 6's answers were unlike everyone else's.

    B) Get all pissed off at Person 6.

    C) Start the initial pattern over again.

    D) Say, "What is this, *Fantasia Part 3!?*"

We prefer "**C**" because now we are armed with an invisible script.

An easy way for this scene to fall apart is to confront Person 6 with a series of Who, What, Where, Why, and How questions.

It doesn't matter who Person 6 is though, because the scene is about:

> A) Donald Duck Walk-Ons, *Circle of Life* sing-a-longs, and *Fantasia* sequels.
> B) A Disney World addiction support group where everyone has serious problems except for one person who has only been once and wants to go back.
>
> C) Jokes about Disney World.
>
> D) All of the above.

The correct answer is "**B**"!

With this, we avoid all Word Association traps, we keep the scene alive by heightening the "thing," and we've got a good central character anchoring the scene.

Gold.

CHAPTER 9

Spatial Relation, Logical Connectives, and Abiogenesis
Using "Dress the Scene" To Help Map Scenes

At our training centers, we use the exercise "Dress the Scene" in our Improv Zero Intro and Level 1 improv classes.

"Dress the Scene" helps us to look at the scene with a different part of our brains in order to see it with a new structure.

It's a super-basic exercise and by no means is it an invention of ours, but we have tweaked it to suit the needs of our improv philosophies.

What we love about it is the opportunity that it gives us to examine scenes piecemeal - to look for smarter, better, more concise choices, to recognize patterns, and to build up to stronger, more inspired ideas.

The Dress the Scene exercise also helps us hardcore pay attention to the Facts that help us determine the Paths of our scenes.

Here we go, Dress the Scene!

EXAMPLE: DRESS THE SCENE

OK, this is a blank stage, blank empty space.

It is our job to fill it.

Like in a real improv scene, in this exercise, we are all adding information to the scene to define what the heck is going on.

However, in "Dressing the Scene," we are doing it "visually" (even though we can't see the objects we create on an improv stage).

We start by creating an object onstage, something that is relatable, something we can all understand.

Our first student approaches the stage and tells us, "There is a row of bunk beds against the wall."

This is our first definitive offer into this new improv world that we will conjure onstage. This is our reference object, the point from which we will measure all of our other objects.

Now, knowing that there are bunk beds - not just one, but a *row of them* - communicates a very specific idea to the improvisers.

We can all agree that this is some kind of communal area, a room used for sleeping, a temporary space, potentially not for adults. We want to connect bunk beds with a thread of logic and narrow the idea further.

The next student offers, "On all of the bunk beds, there are sleeping bags."

Camp. This is probably camp.

No one is shocked when the next student says, "There is a banner over the door that says, '*Welcome to Camp Kickapoo.*'"

Fact!

It's important to connect these first objects tightly with logic, building a strong foundation for the rest of the scene.

If the second offer into the scene (sleeping bags) wasn't as closely related to bunk beds, we might have a more difficult time moving forward together as an ensemble on the same page.

If the second offer is, "There is a window on this wall," we might have a more difficult time getting to the action of the scene quickly.

"Window" also absolutely lives in this world, but it doesn't speak as directly to "bunk bed" as "sleeping bag" does.

So, we have what looks to be The Camp Scene.

Excellent.

We can all relax a little. We know what goes on at camp, we understand the operating rules, we can all agree on Facts associated with "camp".

But what *specifically* is going on in *this* camp? Is this a scene about the campers? About the staff? About the nighttime ghost stories? About the legend of the camp itself?

The next offer into the scene needs to begin an illustration of what exactly is happening in this scene, what is concretely evident - what is the event we have invoked at this camp?

If the next student makes the offer, "There are suitcases under each of the bunk beds," we are still hovering over "Defining Camp."

We can all assume there are suitcases under the beds, that there are tennis shoes lined up at the door, everyone's pillows have their names written on them in marker, etc.

These details are nice to know, but they are nothing new. We might not know *exactly* where the shoes are lined up, but whether they are against that wall or this one, it doesn't affect what's happening in the scene.

We need action!

The next offer into the scene needs to be an active offer, a new fact that solidifies what path we are undeniably on in the camp scene.

The following student tells us, "All the sleeping bags on the bed are camouflage, except one - a fancy pink sleeping bag."

From what we know about the reference object operands of "bunk beds" and "fancy pink sleeping bag among camouflage sleeping bags," we can start to build our truth-value based on these two Facts.

Bust out that material conditional - *if this, then*! We can apply our *If This, Then What* to the Facts in the scene to make an informed leap to action.

We can all agree that:

1. We are at camp.
2. At camp, we sleep in cabins.
3. Cabins are divided up by gender.
4. If there are a majority of camo sleeping bags, we are most likely in a boys' cabin.
5. If there is a pink sleeping bag in the boys' cabin...

...what is the most logical, simplest explanation of this (logic-simple in an improv sense)?

Is this the cabin where the rules have been bent so that one girl can sleep in this cabin?

Or is this a boys' cabin where one boy has a pink sleeping bag?

What's more interesting?

What's more complicated to play with?

Navigating the scene in the first example (the rules have been changed to allow for a girl to stay in this cabin) can get tricky. It may trap some improvisers into wanting to explain why she is here and what happened with her up to this point to "make sense," rather than play with the Facts at hand.

If we go with the second example (this is just another boy's sleeping bag which happens to be pink), we potentially don't have to explain as much.

It makes sense that he is there in the boys' cabin since he is a boy.

The thing that is bringing the action to the scene is the first interesting or unusual thing (pink sleeping bag), the Thing we are all looking for in each of our scenes. Now we just have to embrace this idea and play with it!

We can connect the two ideas "*boys cabin at camp*" and "*pink sleeping bag*" by having a little fun with truth.

Let's continue with this example. As we explore the scene further, everyone adds something new into the scene that hugs this idea:

Above all the camouflage bunk beds, there are posters of cars and baseball players.[1]

Above the pink sleeping bag bed, there is a gold gilt-framed print of Rossetti's *Pia de' Tolomei*.

All of the camouflaged beds are tidily made-up with fresh towels folded on them.

There is a table on which crafts are neatly displayed - neckties and baseball gloves made out of macaroni, beaded friendship bracelets separated into piles of seasonal colors, an Impressionism-style watercolor exquisite corpse with the signatures of 10 boys' names, pressed wildflowers in *Sports Illustrated*.

There is a pile of crudely-written thank-you cards on the pink sleeping bag, reading, "Dear Brian, U rule! Thanx 4 making our beds again, I have never had a bunk mate who was so cool..."

We have built to a place where we can stop the exercise and ask everyone to boil the scene down to a single phrase. While we won't all say exactly the same phrase, we'll all get to the same conceptual result.

---

[1] And there's a poster with both a car *and* a baseball player. It's Lenny Dykstra riding in the backseat of a Chevy Aveo.

118

Boil this scene down: *The Year We All Met Brian the Fancy Kid at Camp*[2].

Let's do another example!

---

[2] "Gayness" - To make the joke that this kid is "gay" because of some antiquated stereotype about how "effeminate (pink sleeping bag) men are gay" is base and limited. The sexuality of this person has NOTHING to do with the scene. We've all heard gay jokes before and they aren't good jokes. They are offensive and dumb. Let's be the change we want to see in the world and celebrate this kid's uniqueness (he just likes the color pink!) instead! It's potentially more interesting, more fun, and funnier to invent new rules for this kid together with the ensemble. THIS is the kid that has a pink sleeping bag, brings framed art to camp, writes tragicomic prose in his camp notebook, AND EVERYONE AT CAMP LOVES IT!

EXAMPLE: DRESS THE SCENE, PART II

The first object created onstage is a fireplace with a big, thick, wooden mantle.

Next, propped up on the mantle is a framed photograph of a man in chainmail, posing with a foam sword.

On the walls, we see a collection of various swords, shields, and obscure antiquated weaponry.

Okay, we've got it. This is most likely the home of a dude who is super into LARPing[3], historical reenactments, or something similar.

Most likely, our thought process goes along this path:

Fireplace and mantle = Living room.

Framed picture of a man in costume = The man is intimately related to this room.

Weapons on the wall = The man in the photo lives here, this is his stuff, as proven by what's suggested in the photo.

Next, what is the event that makes this interesting? What is happening right now that will take us into action and out of a potential List of Funny Things Scene. So far, everything is hugging pretty tightly together.

A student makes a new offer, "There is a laptop open on a table and he is logged into Match.com."

OK - HOLD ON!

We can go one of two directions here. What is the funniest choice?

Do we make this guy some sad "nerd" who is trolling the Internet for a date?

---

[3] This means Live Action Role Playing. We really wanted to add a chapter about what we can all learn from LARPing, but we had to pull it at the last minute because a wizard made us do that.

Or do we make this guy a badass heartthrob?

What has more comedic potential? What has been done before?

Making the Match.com page read, "102,726 unread personal messages," opens funnier doors in this scene than "0 unread personal messages."

If we make this guy a total lady killer, we can then filter "heartthrob hot dude" through "LARPing dude" and render some delightful results.

We can then begin to explore as an ensemble all the ways this guy is a high status badass who scores with the ladies, all the while maintaining a 100% commitment to his medieval warrior personae.

Back to Dressing The Scene:
...we see an open bottle of champagne...
...over here are two heavy, jewel-studded goblets - one with lipstick on it...
...here is a pile of velvet dress fabric crumpled on the floor next to a pile of chainmail...
...we hear the monotonous drone of Gregorian chants just under the moans of a woman whispering "O, Sir Perceval..."

Boil this scene down to a phrase and everyone is pretty thrilled to announce, "LARPer dude gets laid all the time."

Let's let that guy get some! This world we have created is full of "yes" - a world that is so much more ripe for playfulness and exploration than the "no" world.

The "no" world has this dude with "0 personal messages" on his Match.com account, empty pizza boxes, sticky tissues stuffed between the couch cushions, etc. We've seen all this 1,000 times...the "no" world is full of tiny failures.

The "yes" world is full of awesome successes!

Improv gives us the power to breathe life into blank, empty space. We take a few words and ideas, and when we intelligently smoosh them together, we forge a vitality with a voice that's much greater than the sum of its parts.

CHAPTER 10

World's Best Improv Troupe

Many people believe that the 1995-96 Chicago Bulls was and will always be the greatest basketball team ever assembled. They had Michael Jordan (the ultimate alpha-dog) and a great second fiddle in Scottie Pippen. The enigmatic Dennis Rodman did a majority of the dirty work, and the team was flanked with other fantastic role players who, well, knew their roles.

When an improv show fires on all cylinders, it's not unlike a basketball team being on fire.

The main difference here is that the traits described above should never, ever, be restricted to just one person.

One day, we are the alpha-dog and the next we play a smaller role. Sometimes we find ourselves playing second fiddle for several shows in a row and it's very challenging to not let this creep into your subconscious and alter team chemistry.

One night, you are Toni Kukoc and the next night you are Steve Kerr[1].

On our best nights, we are all Michael Jordans.

To paraphrase Detroit Pistons star Isaiah Thomas in Cameron Stauth's *The Franchise,* which was paraphrased in Bill Simmons' *The Book of Basketball,* "It's not about physical skills. Goes far beyond that."

He continues, referencing teams that won a championship one year and then went the opposite direction the next.

---

[1] Toni Kukoc would be good at hosting shows, editing scenes, designing the logo, and booking the tour, while Steve Kerr would be real quiet for most of the scene, but would have really sweet closing lines all the time.

"I read Pat Riley's book, *Show Time*, and he talks about 'the disease of more.' A team wins it one year, and the next year, every player wants more minutes, more money, more shots. And it kills them. It's hard not to be selfish."

In 2007, when Simmons asked Thomas to elaborate on the 1990 book, Thomas said, "The secret of basketball is that it's not about basketball."

This has a lot more to do with improv than you might think. Sure, basketball is a kabillion dollar industry and is seen and played by millions of people a day, while improv isn't nearly as widespread.

But the principles behind a successful NBA team and a successful improv troupe are strikingly similar.

Eye contact.

Listening.

Respect for each other's skill set.

Knowing what people are going to do before they do it.

Teamwork.

Slam dunks.

Air balls[2].

If we take Isaiah's above quote and tweak it for improv, it may read something like this: "It's not about following all of the rules, it goes far beyond that," and then, "Some troupes suffer from the 'disease of more.' A person has one great show, and then the next show they take over and stop listening. Perhaps they are trying to impress somebody in the audience. They stop treating everyone else like a genius and look at themselves as the funniest person in the room."

Playing selfishly won't get you very far.

The World's Best Improv Troupe treats each other the way they want to be treated. They respect each other, they practice LYDO, UBH and YAMF[3].

---

[2] An improv slam-dunk is any scene about farting. An improv air ball is a second scene about farting.

[3] LYDO=Listen Your Dick Off.

UBH = Ultimate Back-Having.

YAMF=Yes And, Mother Fucker.

The Ultimate Back-Having doesn't have a beginning and end; it permeates your life on- and offstage.

They set each other up and pick up the pieces when (if) they fall down. They love what everyone brings to the table, and the show shows it.

Improv is love, and if you don't love one another, the improv won't love you back.

The secret to improv is that it's not about improv.

Another translated quote, this one from Bill Bradley in *Life on the Run* - replacing the word **basketball** with **improv, sport** with **art form,** and **statistics** with **laughs from the crowd:** "Improv, when a certain level of unselfish team play is realized, can serve as a kind of metaphor for ultimate cooperation. It is an **art form** where success, as symbolized by the championship, requires that the dictates of the community prevail over selfish personal impulses. An exceptional player is simply one point on a five-pointed star. **Laughs from the crowd** can never explain the remarkable interaction that takes place on a team."

Eh?

Things That Every Troupe Should Do

Travel to a Large Improv Festival Together

In one night, you could see a popular troupe from a city with rich improv history, then a college group from Small Town, USA. Or a group with famous people in it, followed by a group of people who should be famous.

Go to a festival, watch every show you can, and in the hotel room later that night, talk about all the inspiring things that you saw (good and bad).

And don't fly, drive!

Travel to a Small Improv Festival Together

The Phoenix Improv Festival is big and mighty in its stature, but relatively small on paper, and the festival remains contained in one venue. Everybody will (should) see every show. This leads to some lengthy shoptalk at the after-parties, which is one of our favorite ways to light-speed your development.

One time, we sat and watched TJ Jagadowski and Miles Stroth argue about something. It was incredibly late and everyone was drinking,[4] so while we don't remember the details, we remember our teenage improv brains being riveted.

You don't have to get accepted to the festival to attend - a fast way to liken your troupe to a festival director is to attend all functions as an audience member soaking it in.

---

[4] Improvisers drink a lot at improv festivals. You can make a name for yourself by dominating drinking games like Flip Cup or Ultimate Flip Cup. We made up Ultimate Flip Cup, by the way.
Someone should create this and then invite us to your festival.

Have a Sleepover

As kids, we had sleepovers with our best friends as often as possible. You learn so much about each other and you get to eat cookies straight off the pan.

Doing a great improv show is as much about being comfortable onstage as it is about executing the craft.

Performing with your friends beats performing with strangers any day.

Have sleepovers and eat cookies.

Share what you know.

Get comfortable.

Take a Road Trip to Anywhere Besides an Improv Festival

Your road trip is like one massive ensemble building exercise, so long as everyone doesn't keep their damn headphones on the entire time.

Get in the car and go somewhere.

Anywhere.

Something strange happens when improvisers spend lots of time with other improvisers in a setting where they aren't actually doing any improv.

They become real people around each other.

This is important.

Watch Tape[5]

Film your show and watch it.

It's going to hurt at first, but when you see yourself initiating a scene, the way you stand when you're not onstage, that goofy intro you all spent so much time perfecting, and the look on your scene partner's face when you don't grab the lotion (because clearly *you should have grabbed the lotion right then)*, it'll change things.

---

[5] There's really no debate that watching improv is better when you're live and in the audience. But when an improv show is good on tape, you know it's legit.

As long as it doesn't change your mind about watching the rest of the tape, you'll be better off.

Avoid stopping the tape to talk since everybody has a pen and paper and are writing down all the important talking points.

A good rule of thumb is that whoever takes the most bathroom breaks or has the most doodles on their paper is the most embarrassed at themselves.

If you don't have a coach and you're afraid to tell somebody about the bad habits they're forming (as you should be because giving each other notes can be poisonous), then encourage the group filming session.

In TNM's Training Camp[6] intensives, we watch tape every morning of the previous night's shows and it does wonders for the performers.

Embrace Every Hot Streak

Some of us learn that if we get compliments after a show as an individual, we are "doing it wrong" because "you shouldn't be noticed over the other performers."

There are fundamental flaws in this approach because we naturally gravitate toward the most interesting thing in front of us.

When the coolest guy at the party starts talking about the wild time that crazy thing happened, our attention goes his way.

A good storyteller, though, will engage his audience and make them feel like a part of the journey.

So what about being noticed for your contribution to how your troupe-mates looked onstage? After all, every performer onstage has a stake in the show.

If Jonathan, Margee, and Kaitlin have a killer show and Cyrus clearly didn't, isn't it the collective responsibility of the three to celebrate Cyrus - to pull him off the ground and into the bubble bath with them?

---

[6] We hold Training Camp every summer in both Austin and New Orleans, as well as every winter in New Orleans. There's also a mini-camp at TNM's annual Improv Wins Conference in Austin.

It most definitely is and this show is only as good as the "worst" performance, so perhaps we modify the note to read "if we don't get any compliments after the show, then we are doing it wrong."

Do Mushrooms Together As a Group

WHOA.

Rehearse

This is a no-brainer and all, but some troupes feel like they don't need to rehearse.

Well, they do.

Rehearsing is just as important as the shows that happen afterwards.

Hang Out After Rehearsal

The more regular interaction we have with our troupe-mates, the better we read them, the more we pick up on their sense of humor, the more we learn about their background, the better our scenes become.

Simple!

Things That Every Troupe Should Consider Not Doing

Give Each Other Notes

Once, there was an improv troupe that prided themselves on not having a coach. It was frequently mentioned (by them) on the local improv message boards and even listed in the troupe's bio on their website. They were open and honest with one another, and if someone denied someone's idea, then after the show, they would discuss.

One day, someone finally didn't agree with a note (or at least said out loud for the first time that they didn't agree) and stormed out of the theater. Another person chased after her and the other two remained uncomfortable in the theater.

Also they were dating.

Giving someone notes on their improv is about Status.

You wouldn't hire someone who was lower Status than you (in the improv world) to give *you* notes, so when someone on your troupe offers up a way for you to get better, it often doesn't sit well with the recipient.

The exceptions to this are when someone makes such a bone-headed move (clearly missing an obvious callback or edit, perhaps) that his troupe-mates can't help but call him out on it (even though he's beating himself up over it already) or husband/wife improv troupes.

To avoid all of this, hire an improv coach. And if you refuse to hire a coach, the least you can do is watch your shows on tape in hope that you can see for yourself where you need to improve.

And of course, the longer a group performs together, the more mature and comfortable they become and the more likely it is that they don't need a coach.

Sex, And

Is someone in your troupe sleeping with someone else in your troupe?

Did it happen more than once?

Is it still happening?

Would he or she do it again?

Does anyone know about it?

Are they keeping it a secret?

Will someone find out?

How in the world can we ever be in a comedy troupe if you guys are sleeping together?

When do we bring this up?

How much better would we be if those two people weren't sleeping together?

Everybody panic[7]!

Exclude People from Meetings

If there is a problem with someone in the troupe, then here's a novel concept: Sit down with everyone and talk it out like adults.

Going behind people's backs will only make the problem worse.

Improvisers are notoriously sensitive. Be big boys and girls.

Also, karma is very real.

Count Scenes

You were in the first scene and Walked On to the second. The third begins with a blank stage.

Some may hold back because this would be appearance number three in as many scenes.

Counting scenes could get you in trouble.

The only people who know exactly how many scenes they were in at the end of the night are people who don't have their mind on the improv (and crazy math wizards).

---

[7] Wanting to sex someone in your troupe isn't uncommon.

Here are some tips to express your desires:

1. Initiate lots of scenes where your character wants to sleep with his or her character.

2. If your wishful sexual partner is in a scene with any mention of sex or love with a troupe-mate, then walk on to that scene as his or her husband or wife.

3. Be generally unsupportive of his or her actual boyfriend or girlfriend at all times.

4. Create a side project where it's just the two of you. Rehearse often by yourselves.

Sulk After a Good Show

It's significantly more offensive for a performer to be down on his or her performance after a quality show. You may mean well, but the right move here is to put the group ahead of yourself, thus celebrating the ensemble.

Stack Up on Side Projects

Somebody in your troupe is bound to get invited to join another group, so how do you handle this?

After all, you're working hard to develop a group mind and now someone is spending some of their precious time with another troupe, developing a group mind with *them?*

It may feel like you're being cheated on. You may feel like the group is weaker.

Here, we encourage you to take a page from Mr. Mick Napier and take care of yourself. There is nothing wrong with spreading your wings, baby bird. Just remember to keep your priorities straight and loyalties in line.

People who get involved in lots of side projects are just satisfying their own needs because they aren't creatively fulfilled in their "main" troupe or because they're incredibly ambitious. (Although it's probably the former, not the latter.)

Do Mushrooms Together As a Group

Seriously: Whoa.

Make T-Shirts and Buttons Before Your First Show

Your intensity is remarkable, it really is!

We hate to say no to something so soon, but perhaps you should put your efforts into becoming a tighter group instead of making t-shirts and buttons.

You don't want to be that group with the really slick marketing, but nothing onstage to back it up, right?

Freak Out Over a Troupe Name

Your first fight is probably going to be over your troupe's name. In the best-case scenario, your name arrives organically through a troupe-wide inside joke or a badass group scene.

Our favorite example came during a new troupe casting call. A group scene emerged where people were attending a ghost prom.

It was big, it was funny, it involved everyone onstage. Once the troupe was officially formed, the name Ghost Prom was suggested and everyone immediately agreed.

Easiest name selection process of all time!

It might not work out so perfectly for you, so here's our handy-dandy guide to your troupe-naming process:

- Start an online document that everyone has access to.
- For a week, everyone is allowed to add however many names to the list as they want. Bonus points for names that are inspired by scenes the group has performed.
- Then everyone meets up and sits in a circle. Each member is allowed to take a name off the list (maybe more if the list is long) without having to defend their choice. If one person on the group doesn't like a name, then it has to go.
- Everyone then secretly picks their three favorite names, and every name that doesn't get mentioned is eliminated.
- Hopefully we're left with less than ten names at this point.
- We do a second round of no-explanation-needed eliminations and then you vote.

Bam! Slightly complicated, but fun.

Also, for a list of every single improv troupe name that hasn't been taken yet, check the secret Bonus Chapter at the end of this book. There are plenty of good ones still available for choosing!

CHAPTER 11

Everything But the Show

It's not hard to find someone with an opinion on scene work in improv. People read one book on improv, bump one argument on some message board, and take two months of classes and they think they're the next Del Close.

However, people don't usually spend much time breaking down the intricacies of what surrounds the scene work.

Everything from arriving to the show, your behavior backstage once the lights drop, and how you party at the after-party can be part of this big magical world of improv, too.

The Day of the Show

Everything from the food you eat to the music you listen to matters, since it could dictate your mental state heading into a performance.

Does eating before a show make you nauseous?

Does performing on an empty stomach distract you?

Will listening to a certain song increase your energy level?

Do you need complete silence to gather your thoughts?

Does it matter how many people are out there in the crowd?

Are you checking?

Is saying out loud to one another, "I've got your back," going to help you remember to support each other, or is it just something you say because you've always said it?

Do you say it long before the show starts or at the last minute?

We suggest that you find out.

Work through these rituals before every show. Try out different warm-ups. Take turns being the leader and then follow that leader.

And don't be the last one to the theater.

Warming Up

Many people need to perform a specific exercise so they feel more confident executing the lesson of said exercise ("We need to be high-energy for this show, so let's play Crazy 8's!" or "The more eye contact we make, the better our scenes are, so let's do some Mirroring!")

In lieu of exercises at your next rehearsal, run as many "shows" as time allows, attempting to duplicate the pre-show feeling and experiment with your showtime rituals.

Perhaps you'll discover something new!

Most groups with a couple of years under their belt have a stock group of warm-ups that they always run.

But what happens if someone is running late[1] and your ritual doesn't take place?

The more experienced the group, the less this matters, which begs the question, how much does it matter in the first place?

For some, not at all.

Our friend Brian O'Connell (iO Theatre, Los Angeles) says:

"Personally, I don't believe in warming up. I think your day is your warm-up. If I'm feeling down or confused about my life, I'll use that energy as a force for good in the show.

I think a better way to approach warming up is to connect for a few moments ahead of time with your teammates.

Ask how their day was before they saw you. Did they learn anything new? Make eye contact. Be present. Let everybody feel like the other people in the room care about them and want to be involved.

I don't need forced games to get my eye contact down with my teammates. I'd rather make a real, human connection, just for a moment, to remind them and myself why we play together in the first place: We enjoy each other as artists and as friends.

---

[1] It's okay if you're a little late, but just don't be the last one to arrive.

So, let's skip the bullshit and just go out and put that in front of an audience.

For others, warming up is a sacred tradition.

Jose Gonzalez (The Torch Theatre, Phoenix) says:

"Personally, I'm a fan of warming up, especially for using physicality. I find that, without stretching and getting a good physical- and movement-based warm-up, I tend to be pretty stiff and talking heady in my scenes.

In general, I think if anyone in a group expresses a desire to warm-up in some way, it's a good idea to support them and have a good chunk of warming up before hitting the stage.²"

Our favorite warm-ups are the ones that are organically created by the group.

This one, from Stupid Time Machine in New Orleans, is called "Tell Us What You Do For Your Man," as explained by CJ Hunt (The New Movement, New Orleans).

"Like many rhythmic or melodic warm-ups, you really have to hear people playing "Tell Us What You Do For Your Man" in order to get the hang of it. Nonetheless, we will try to give you a taste here:

> *The group stands in a circle and begins a steady rhythmic clap, much like you would clap along with the beat at a concert.*
> *The group chants:*
> *"Tell us ... Whatcha do for yo man..."*
> *"Tell us ... Whatcha do for yo man..."*
> *Then the first player in the circle responds:*
> *"My man really likes it when I...[blank blank blank blank]."*

---

² We definitely agree with this, unless it's the same person every time suggesting that you play Big Booty over and over again.

Then all bets are off and this person should not be taken seriously.

Here, the individual names a mundane or absurd action that their man supposedly enjoys in a sexy way like, "My man really likes it when I clip them coupons."

While saying it, the individual player pantomimes doing whatever activities he or she is singing about. The group then joins in the pantomime while singing:

"Oooooo, you like that shit?"

"Ooooo, you wanna get with this?"

(Repeat and move to the next player in the circle)"

The New Movement has a mega-successful weekly all-star show called "The Megaphone Show."

So how does the all-star cast get prepared?

The warm-ups for this show often consist of one long, fluid, organic scene that may see someone pull out a skateboard and implore for everyone to ride it, only to see the skateboard turn into a hot air balloon and everyone happens to be deathly afraid of heights so everyone grips each other tightly chanting, "It'll be okay. It'll be okay," which morphs into, "Middle the day," which morphs into, "Griddle to stay," and we all end up protesting our right to keep our griddle until someone looks at their watch[3] and realizes it's time to do a show.

It's nothing at all, but it means everything because it gets everyone on the same page.[4] It's infectious, and that's an important word to use when describing a warm-up.

So is warming up for a show simply a case of "doing a bunch of scenes" or "being in the mental space of an improv show?"

Is it just a matter of hanging out with the people you're about to be onstage with?

And how much time are we willing to put into warming up?

Isn't it easier to just show up and perform?

---

[3] Or until the laser bomb explodes.

[4] Bonus: anyone within earshot gets to experience an array of emotions.

Again, we suggest that you find out! Your next show is likely not your last,[5] so try something new[6].

1 or 100

You're ready to go, and it's almost showtime. You peak through the curtain or you crack the door to get a glimpse of the audience.

In a perfect world, the theater is packed with smart, improv-appreciative people for every single show.

Real talk, this isn't always the case.

Before you sneak peek, ask yourself, is the size of the crowd really going to determine whether or not you're striving to make the smartest choices?

If that guy you just started dating didn't show up, are you going to forget how to initiate a scene?[7]

We like the One or One-Hundred Theory. We're doing the same show, regardless of who's in the building.

Yeah, the energy that comes from a hundred people can definitely fuel a show, but your primary source of inspiration should be the art of improv itself, so if there's one person watching, how about giving that person the time of their life?[8]

---

[5] Don't worry. We're knocking on wood for you.

[6] Your warm-up might depend on the type of show you're about to do. If it's a duo, eye contact and hang-out time will suffice.

A new troupe will want to pull out the comfortable classics (likely in the presence of a coach).

A reuniting troupe will talk about each other's kids and divorces.

An "All Star" troupe will be using the bathroom, checking texts, and wandering around the lobby, waiting for the show to start.

[7] We suggest the initiating line: "Honey, you missed my improv set. I think we should break up."

[8] When we first opened The New Movement, we refused to cancel a show, even if there was only one person in the audience and it was a student.

It's bad form.

The show goes on and the show will totally rule.

The Tech Booth

It's about thirty minutes until showtime. Has there been any communication between you and the tech booth?

If you have specific tech needs, then you'll want to outline them clearly for the person in the booth.

Or hey, maybe you have your own tech person!

Even if you don't have specific tech needs, then you'll still want to talk to them so that they don't do something like the following:

- Use the booth microphone to be part of your show whenever they feel like it.
- Incorporate sound effects to be thunder or rain or Ace of Base.
- Dip the lights up and down so that you (and now the entire audience) know that they are looking for an edit to end the show.
- Play the next song on their playlist as your intro music, which could be something real un-fun like "Uninvited" by Alanis Morissette, instead of playing a song that you specifically requested. If you're playing in unfamiliar territory, you should definitely bring your own intro music, or at least say the words, "Please bring us out to something that's high energy".[9]

---

[9] **True Stories with Christopher Michael:** Once, I gave a sound guy at an improv festival a CD. The CD had nothing on it (my mistake, I intended to burn our intro song. Hence the label "INTRO SONG".)

We were announced with no music, so we waited backstage. Waited. And waited. Finally, we emerged to some weird energy.

After the show, I asked the sound guy what happened, and he was all, "Oh, your CD had nothing on it."

Thanks!

"I've Got Your Back."

Right before you hit the stage is usually the time when everyone whispers, "I've got your back."

You have to do this because if you don't, then you wouldn't remember to support each other.

For a lot of people, saying, "I've got your back," makes them feel like they've already done so.

Show don't tell. Or, tell if you really want to. Not a big deal, unless you never come through.

We prefer eye contact and something genuine.

The Opening Spiel

How will the host introduce you? Have you talked to them yet?

We recommend you do, so that any awkward moments can be avoided and you can look your best.

Your accomplishments sound better when they come from a third party.

"Hi, we're The Cat Dunkers and we've been to over a dozen improv festivals and were once named Sacramento's Best Improv Troupe. Can we get a suggestion," doesn't sound nearly as badass as, "Ladies and gentlemen, please welcome to the stage a group that's been to over a dozen improv festivals and were once named Sacramento's Best Improv Troupe...The Cat Dunkers!"[10]

Arriving Onstage

This is the audience's first impression of you. Make sure and have a game plan, even if it's just, "We walk out and stand in a line and then Mandy says hi."

---

[10] If someone names their troupe The Cat Dunkers, we'll invite you to our next big festival.

The more unified you look, the better you'll feel. Take this seriously, especially since performing smart improv is hard when you feel uncomfortable and everything traces back to the beginning.

If you've been improvising for less than a year, chances are you've at least considered doing a scripted introduction like one of these actual introductions we've seen before:

- Terrorize the audience with fake guns and knives, demanding that they give you a suggestion.
- Spit water into the crowd like a pro wrestler, inevitably getting someone wet who didn't want to get wet.
- Pretend to be throwing a surprise party for someone, and the only gift they want is a suggestion.
- A pre-written rap song that precedes an improvised musical.
- Explain the intricacies of your format to an audience of people that have likely never taken an improv class.
- Everyone shouts the name of the troupe at the same time.

If having a scripted introduction makes you feel good, then we encourage you to do this!

Eventually, though, you'll grow out of it and you'll focus on getting yourself mentally prepared to do funny scene work, and you won't stress out about an opening.

Post-Show Stuff

The Closing Spiel

The lights drop and it's time to say goodnight.

What you do next, when the lights come up, says a lot about your troupe and how they felt about the show.

If you scatter like roaches, then something went wrong.

If everyone stands up straight with satisfied looks on their faces, then something went right.

If everyone is suddenly wearing each other's clothes, and one person puts their arms through another person, taking the place of *their* arms, then something went wacky.

Holding hands and taking a bow isn't completely necessary, unless you're doing a real complicated format[11] that you're proud of. If you're going to do this, we recommend practicing it.

If nobody steps forward to end your set, then you either have no leader or you're disorganized.

If someone steps up and recites a list of things for the audience to do (check out our website, take our classes, inside joke #1, follow and like us on social networks, happy birthday to that person, inside joke #2, our next show is in March, if you liked us, tell a friend, if you didn't, we were the Blue Man Group), then you're asking for too much.

Since you were so mind-blowingly brilliant, people will probably Google you later anyway. Pick two and say goodnight.

Hanging Out

Is there something more to your troupe than the show? Are you hosting a fundraiser next week, or do you teach classes, or are you selling t-shirts?

If so, then you'd better be hanging out after your show where people can find you.

Look them in the eye and thank them. Hand them a flier, if you have one.

A lot of improv folks might want to stay in the green room. Or you guys really connected, and something beautiful happened onstage, so we get why'd you want some private time.

---

[11] Some examples: Improvised Street Fighter II, Improvised Great Depression, Improvised Harry Potter, Improvised Golden Girls, Improvised Improv, Improvised Dinosaurs the TV show (Not the Momma).

Building a fan-base is much easier when you're accessible. The person who approaches you after the show to tell you how much they laughed is the same person who is going to buy your album, follow you on social networks, and support your next big event.[12]

The After-Party

Bars are great, but if you really want to enable some all-night shop-talk, you gotta go to a place where there are as few non-improvisers as possible.

This is usually someone's house. Feel free to take some you-lovin' audience members along, but only if they're comfortable with non-stop jokes and scene breakdowns.[13]

At the party, count on the following things to happen:

1. The crazy guy gets naked.
2. Someone you didn't know had a substance-abuse problem will abuse a substance or three.
3. For every ten people present, three new troupes will form. Fifteen percent of these troupes will actually do a show someday (but only one show).
4. Warm-ups will constantly be in play and the neighbors will get pissed.
5. Someone will say, "It's not like I'm trying to be Tina Fey or anything, but still…"

---

[12] **True Stories with Christopher Michael:** I once performed with a guy who said things like, "I'm going to go stand outside to see if I can get some compliments." (This is not the right approach.)

[13] If you bring your non-improviser significant other to more than three improv parties a month, they will either break up with you or come up with reasons to not attend shows, which will cause you to eventually break up with them.

Or they will start taking improv classes.

Talking to the Press

Sometimes, we do a good enough job to get some ink in the local newspaper.

This is awesome because the more good words we can spread about improv, the better.

The general public still doesn't seem to totally get the idea of long-form, so the stakes are high for your interview. Some suggestions, please[14]:

1. Don't even mention *Whose Line Is It, Anyway.*

If you're still describing your improv troupe by saying what it's not, then that's too bad.

Let's pretend that this world is as unfamiliar with music as it is with improv, and you play in the Sex Pistols. Referencing *Whose Line Is It, Anyway* is like the press asking you to describe what your music is like and you responding with, "Are you familiar with Nursery Rhymes? Yeah, we're kinda like those."

Also, *Whose Line Is It, Anyway* is a pretty outdated reference, Urkel.

2. Your jokes aren't going to be nearly as funny in print.

That line about "improv getting you laid" wasn't really that funny in your head or on the phone, and it's way worse in print.

The most important thing to remember when talking to the press is Save The Jokes For The Stage. You are probably interesting and funny enough without making overt jokes, and the press will pick up on that.

Relax and don't try so hard!

---

[14] Female circumcision.

3. If you say something hack like, "Improv is the most fun you'll ever have with your clothes on," then you are a creep.

Gross.

Let the press interview someone else in your group.

4. Be humble, be nice.

You know it's super annoying to read interviews with smug assholes who speak as if they are the first goofball to be interviewed by the press.

So be the change you want to see in the world. Being likeable, honest, and humble will probably make more fans than detaching yourself from your audience and talking over them.

CHAPTER 12

No Suggestion Needed

We stopped taking suggestions for our shows when we started The New Movement in 2009.

Traditionally, a suggestion is taken at the top of an improv show as proof that the show was improvised and not previously written.

We borrowed from two of our favorite improvisers TJ & Dave, the "Trust Us This Is All Made Up" approach - without literally saying as much.

While on our first "Chris and Tami Tour," we experimented with different ways of connecting with the audience from the moment we were onstage.

Most people who came to see our shows had no idea who we were. Because we have an insanely powerful marketing machine, we were able to fill large houses in cities we'd never visited, based on little to no audience knowledge of our reputation.

People simply knew we were touring improv comics who knew the right folks in town who could book a good show (and we had cool-looking posters).

But we knew how high the stakes were during those shows. The audience had no reason to like us, so we had to earn their approval and validate their choice immediately.

But how do you win over an audience immediately?

First, let's talk about what doesn't work - or what didn't work for us, at least.

Coming out onstage with a planned opening,[1] or some super funky, high-energy dancing, or acting too cool and unapproachable serve to cut an immediate division between the audience and us.

Consequently, we often felt like the first few scenes of our show became a breathless tap dance to win back the people we alienated with our assault of an opening.

We started to feel that planning an opening and taking a suggestion were more awkward than helpful as an introduction or a springboard into fresh ideas.

While on tour, we were performing in fairly new improv markets, and many of our audiences were not used to being commanded to shout out random words.

In the past, we had used certain approaches to try to coax the audience to say something, anything, by leading them into a suggestion - "What's your favorite thing to do on a weekend?" - but it never felt fluid.

More often than not, there would be an uncomfortable few moments of silence before some brave soul would whimper, "Camping?" And then we'd get right into our first scene "inspired" by camping.

What we knew for a fact at that time: To have a good show, your first impression on the audience must be that you're *likable*, a confoundedly complicated thing to achieve in 10 seconds.

How do you be likable!?

Our new approach was to dial it all back and keep the opening and introduction to our shows SIMPLE.

With The New Movement, we decidedly, passionately abandoned suggestions all together.

Play high-energy, fun music to come out to.

Hit the stage smiling, standing at the lip of the stage and clapping with the audience.

---

[1] Planned Openings for Improvised Shows started to feel ingenious and mismatched in the whole of the performance. It's a confusing message to the audience, in our opinion. Simple, short openings are totally cool. Long, complicated openings are not.

We use these first precious moments onstage to establish a trust with the audience.

We come out onstage and *smile.*

We thank the audience for coming.

We introduce the show and ourselves, and we treat them like friends by telling them exactly what is up with us.

"Hi! We are Chris and Tami and we are excited to do a show for you right now."

We try our best to be honest and true and real and relatable. And likable, which for us, was obtained by simply exhibiting to the audience that we are comfortable onstage, that we have a great relationship with each other, that we love what we are doing, and that they don't have to worry about anything uncomfortable happening.

And it works.

We never lack for inspiration to start our show, we never have anyone doubt our show is improvised[2].

The students of The New Movement don't take suggestions for classes or shows.

They've never needed to.

We have such a wealth of information bubbling up to our subconscious to pull from at all times - the weird phone call you got this morning, that annoying lady at the bank, your boss' confusing facial tick, the dream you had last night.

Once we challenge ourselves to pull from this information, we are training ourselves to be more honest more quickly onstage.

When we believe that ANYTHING can be inspiring, everything is.

---

[2] OK, fine. Sometimes when an audience is TOTALLY unfamiliar with improv, we'll have the disbelievers approach us with doubtful eyes, berating us with, "NONE of that was written? But how'd you know that he was the guy from the airplane? You didn't plan ANY OF THAT?"

But that's a wonderful compliment and only comes from folks introduced to improv by our shows.

CHAPTER 13

Take Your Uninspired Ass Here

It's okay if you feel uninspired from time to time. Improv is hard, and getting really good at improv is *really* hard.

This sort of thing happens to everyone, so it's okay!

However, it's not okay for you to mope about it.

We're here to help you get out of your slump.

We designed this chapter to be revisited whenever you're in need of inspiration.

Remember that every rehearsal, class, jam, or show has the potential to pick you up from the ground, brush the dirt off your back, and have you feeling sky-high.

Okay...so what's wrong?

You had a bad show.

All right, we're sorry to hear about it, but so what? Improv is a delicate dance, and sometimes it doesn't go as planned.

Maybe you were in a rush to make call time?

Maybe you need a different pre-show ritual?

Or maybe you just had one bad show!

Remember that we have to have bad shows to know how to have good shows.

Take it as a lesson and move on.

Listen to the universe.

150

If you've had three bad shows in a row and you had a pulled pork sandwich before each of them, then blame it on the pulled pork[1] and get excited about rehearsal tonight. And don't eat no pulled pork sandwiches before rehearsal!

Your ideas keep getting turned down.

We know.

It's weird because we're all floating in a big, shiny pool of Yes, but the truth is that not everyone is going to love your ideas all the time.

Especially if you're the one in the group who keeps having all of them.

It hurts when nobody in your immediate creative circle gets on board with you, but instead of sulking, we suggest you sleep on it. If you wake up in the morning and you still want to do that weird thing with the crazy outfit and the silly intro, then give your idea a name and invite some people to play along.

It may be weird when the original naysayers catch wind of your new project, but this isn't about them. It's about you and what inspires you.

Now go, young lion, go!

You did mushrooms and you realize that you're madly in love with someone in your troupe.

Whoa. Okay, calm it down.

---

[1] The worst things for you to eat before a show, in order:

5. Tub of ice cream and yogurt mix

4. Cinnamon bread from Domino's Pizza (without frosting)

3. Chili-covered hamburger

2. Paper

1. Cinnamon bread from Domino's Pizza (with frosting)

This is going to be weird for a while, but you've got some time. No need to rush into anything right now.

Here's what you do:

Apply to an out-of-town improv festival where he/she has a friend, and then encourage your improv troupe to travel there and stay in a hotel together.

Be sure to book a hotel room that plays on a discomfort in his/her world (i.e. If she's allergic to smoke, book a smoking room).

On the first or second night of the festival, mention how you think you are also maybe kind of allergic to smoke, and doesn't he/she have a friend who lives in this city?

Maybe y'all can stay there?

Do so, and then the next morning, miss your flights on purpose and have more fun together.

Next, take him/her on the most elaborate date possible, preferably in some other exotic town.

Once you start official dating, plan four separate parties to celebrate his/her birthday, replete with road trips and picnic baskets and thoughtful callbacks to the old days when you were only troupe-mates.

Quit your jobs.

Invest everything in each other.

Start a new theater and improv conservatory together.[2]

Everyone else wants the same logo/form/whatever and you don't like it.

This is a common problem with an easy solution: SPEAK UP!

If you allow an idea to snowball, the people who came up with the idea will dig their heels further into the ground.

If something doesn't feel right, say it out loud before the rest of the group gets too excited.

---

[2] When all of that is complete, write a book about improv together.

The same person in your troupe keeps getting all the attention.[3]

This is a tough one.

Is he/she enjoying a hot streak, or has this been the case from day one?

If you're the jealous type and this has been going on for a while, you've got two choices here. You can either use this discomfort as self-motivation, and devote yourself to becoming the best performer you can be, or you can let your insecurities grow into a big, mean monster.

Big, mean monsters don't really belong in improv, so if you find yourself heading down this path, you should see a psychologist or get a new hobby.

If it's just a hot streak that they're enjoying, then relax. Hot streaks come and go in improv, so sleep calm knowing that yours is on its way.

You can expedite the process by treating people the way you want to be treated. The universe will reward this!

Also, that person getting all the attention all the time probably isn't thinking about it as much as you are.

You and that guy/girl in the group aren't getting along lately.

Is it a fight-fight or just a fight?

Can you see yourself performing improv without this person?

---

[3] Our friend Shyla Ray, TNM graduate and founder of The Station in Houston, says: "In improv, you have to think of yourself like a Transformers combiner (a super transformer comprised of several Transformers), or a Viking horde.

Your strength is a direct result of with whom you have united. Iron sharpens Iron. If your troupe-mate gets lots of attention, learn from them. Also, jealousy comes from distance, so get closer to that person. Bask in being on the same team as someone worthy of you, and focus on being the best team possible!"

Do you actively wish that this person wasn't around, because that makes you a better performer?

Creative disagreements are very real, but if handled correctly, won't leave permanent scars.

If you've read these paragraphs a couple of times over because you're wondering if this is you, we suggest you talk to your coach first. He or she will likely have some insight on the matter, and you'll be back on the road to success.

It may be a rough gravel-y road at first, but communication will put you on smooth ground faster than you can say "great metaphor."[4]

Someone is late/drunk/high/mean/sleepy all the time.

Pull this person aside and tell them how it makes you feel. If they don't stop, then talk to the group.

A personal conflict like this doesn't need to go through a coach, but it can if you're a scared-y cat. The game of this situation is to solve the problem as fast as possible. Do not allow the character to heighten.

Everyone in class knows how to do that new thing and you don't.

This ain't no biggie if it's only happened a few times.

People take to different concepts in different ways. Don't be so hard on yourself.

If this is becoming a pattern, talk to your teacher. Tell them that you're struggling and ask if there is anything you can do outside of class to work on the new concept.

---

[4] Thanks! Did you understand what we meant by "gravel-y"? We almost went with rocky road, but we didn't want to get anyone confused with the footnote a couple pages back.

Any improv teacher worth their salt should easily be able to offer some advice or encouragement here.

At the very least, being truthful about your problems will help you overcome it. No great improviser ever becomes great with zero struggles on their stat sheet.

Open the box!

You don't get along with your teacher.

If you only have to deal with them for another seven weeks, then bite your tongue and hang on tight.

If this teacher will be your teacher again (because they are in charge of the conservatory or because the staff is small), then maybe you should seek out a different training center. Especially if the teacher is instilling fear and doubt in you and showing no signs of encouragement.

Or maybe this is when you focus up[5], learn all you can, and then open your own training center, vowing to never use these same tactics.

---

[5] Focus up. Never forget this.

Things You Can Do By Yourself to Get Better at Improv

Detect Patterns

Pull some items out of your kitchen pantry, then try to line them up in a pattern.

Maybe it's the "Things that require butter" pattern or the "Dogs love this" pattern. See how many different combinations you can come up with.

That can of black beans is the initiating line, so what is the most logical path to follow?

Refried beans? Simple and to the point!

Oh wait, the second beat is diced tomatoes! That's more complex![6]

Imagine Character Monologues

You're stuck in traffic.

Luckily, so is the person next to you. Be their inner thoughts, adopt their posture, and talk like you think they talk for as long as the traffic light is red.

This also works at bus stops, but you have to do it all in your head.

Kinda.

Listen

Pay attention to characters out in the real world!

Study how they walk and move. Take some inspiration from them. All improvisers probably do this already, but see what happens when you really get into it.

---

[6] Having a hard time holding back unleashing five more pages on this.

How much of a conversation can you remember? How can you use it in a scene?

Play Chess

Good chess players are able to think several moves ahead. The bishop is there, but only because the knight is about to go there, which will make your queen go there, which is about to get ganked by this rook.

In this world, everything means something.

Listen to Rap Music

Rappers are really good at feeling good.

Whatever your favorite rap album is, listen to it some more. Discover (and maintain) your swagger.

If you don't have a favorite rap album, you better find one.[7]

Watch or Read Something

You may already be a TV geek or movie buff, and you may have, like, billions of books, but try watching or reading something like an improviser would.

If you were playing that character, what would you do?

How would you play that character onscreen?

Entertain Yourself...

...with a one-person improv show.

Lock the door, silence your phone, and draw the curtains. Play all the characters and use sweep edits.

Don't look at the clock. Just go!

---

[7] Rappers also have multiple ways of saying the same exact things, a quality definitely applicable to improv. And they are permanently high-status!

Write It Down[8]

Put your ideas on paper and share it with your troupe-mates or students. Post it on a relevant message board for feedback.

You may develop a new exercise or school of thought along the way!

---

[8] A few other books we wish we had time to write:
How to Win TV's Survivor
Improv and Animal Training
Re-Writing Professional Wrestling from 2002 to Today

CHAPTER 14

Thank You and Goodnight

Raise your glasses!

Here's to YOU (person who helped us, supported us, loved us, came to all of our parties)!

Let The Comedy Juggernaut Proceed!

Thanks from Chris Trew:

Thanks, Ryan Ramos, for saying to me on the set of VH1's *Motormouth* in 2004 that I should take an improv class.

Thanks, Mom and Dad, for not freaking out about me selling my car to go to Chicago for a summer intensive and also for constantly repeating the "treat people the way you want to be treated" mantra.

Thanks, Joe Canale, Steve Waltein, and TJ Jagadowski for being my favorite performers that summer and for remembering me as the dude who always sat in the front row.

Thanks, Brock LaBorde, for helping with the production of this book and for being my comedy partner in crime since 2001. Thank goodness you're editing this book, so you can make me say nice things about you to the whole world, like how you have the coolest face that anyone's ever seen.

Thanks from Tami Nelson:

Feodora Mae Kennedy Scott for always laughing at my jokes and making it possible for me to detach from the matrix and do comedy full-time. Mom for not freaking out when I did that and always supporting me, following the fun.

Jay Vickers for always making me feel like the funniest person alive and lending me $100 to take my first improv class.

Thanks from both of us:

Shyla Ray for being the brave pioneer, supporting us, and helping to get TNM off the ground early on.

Christie Grace, Sarah Price, Paul Sontag, Brian Boyko, and **Patrick Knisely** for trusting us and coming along for the ride.

Clay Barton for being our pal in business for a while and play for all time.

Derek Dupuy, Mike Spara, CJ Hunt, and Grace Blakeman for being our feet on the ground in NOLA, making it possible for us to move back to the city we love and expand TNM and make New Orleans a destination for comedy in the south.

Vanessa Gonzales, Michael Foulk, Alex Berry, Dan Grimm, and Amy Jordan for taking the reigns on TNM Austin, making it possible for us to move back to the city we love and expand TNM.

Mona Lee for having Chris substitute teach an improv class for actors when he had never taught improv in his life before because that's where he met Kristen Tucker.

Kristen Tucker for being like, "You guys should teach improv, you're really good at it," which made us be like, "Let's look into this."

Everyone who's ever given us a ride for giving us rides. We don't have a car.

Mick Napier for writing the first improv book that made a lot of sense to us and that was instrumental in our early development.

J* for letting us crash in that weird room with all the America shit on three different tours.

Uncle Joe Bill for supporting us, being excited about us, and being a cool uncle to party with.

Alex Woodward, Chris Sherrod, Justin Strackany, Brady James, Sam Stites, Christy Lorio, Jessica Brown, Sean Brightman, Chadwick Smith, Lindsay Adkins, for donating to this book's Kickstarter and for choosing the reward to have your name live on forever right here and elsewhere in this book. You directly helped this book become a reality.

Everyone else - We are incredibly lucky to know so many interesting and amazing people. Thank you for being a part of this thing we're all building together.

We love you.

Improv is the Winner.

BONUS CHAPTER

Available Troupe Names

We believe that these are the only troupe names still available as of the date of this book's publishing (today).

Montanabama
Let's Make a Stew
~~Claws with Fangs~~
This Is Happening
Groovy Automotive
Bassprov
Prov Unit E: Miami
Bananas in Pajamas
~~Handbomb~~
50 Cent presents: Vitamin Water
Larry's Good Time
Land and Swim
Jay Herrod
The Fart Whisperers
Tomzilla
The Wallflounders
Big Momma's House Team Players
Neighborhood Swatch
Guitar Gyro
Netgear
One Man Short
Decent Space Unit
Spirited Desiree'
Semen
The Cat Dunkers

~~Brows~~
Free Willy Wonka and the Chocoholics Music Factory
Blame it on the Stain
200 Degrees: Hot Hot Improv
Comedy? Provably.
Arms Expert Anonymous
Gross Prom
The Control Troupe
One Hand Clapping
Improvalaya
~~Dean's List~~
Yummy Provalicious
Spaghetti and Improv: Oops, we meant Meatballs!
IMPortant PROVclamation
IMPty Nest Syndrome
IMPterior: House
Around the Horn
Whites Only
Blink 185
~~Opposites~~
Ducktales But Not Ducktales
The Hermaphro-Lites
The Just Clownin's
Tuesday Shuffle
The Mushroom Tips
AMF: America's Funniest Ladies!
The Snowcone Kids
Hurley's Fat Stomach
Snick at Nite
The Har-Har-vard Sailing Squad
Tee-Hee-Man & The Masters of the Universe
~~Art Camp~~
Grandma's Buttplug
Branson, Missouri
The Junktown Wackies
Show Me the Funny!

Every **January** in **Austin, Tx**

An education conference and festival

improvwins.com to register

**The biggest comedy
event in the Gulf South**

HELLYES FEST

Every **November** in
New Orleans, La

hellyesfest.com

MULTIPLE
CITIES

MULTIPLE
WEEKENDS

THE COMEDY EVENT OF THE SUMMER

THE
MEGAPHONE
MARATHONS

megaphonemarathons.com

Twitter: @ImprovWins

Instagram: Improv_Wins

Facebook.com/improvwins

About the Authors

Chris Trew and Tami Nelson live in New Orleans, Louisiana, teaching and performing regularly at their home base of The New Movement.

Chris is an actively touring comedian, traveling around the US with standup and improv tours, as well as with the Air Sex World Championships. Chris can also be seen monthly in Austin as his wrestling manager personae ChrisTrew.biz with Anarchy Championship Wrestling.

Tami teaches all entry-level classes (Levels 1 and 2) at TNM NOLA. She also coaches student and house troupes and performs with a variety of projects at TNM.

Chris and Tami produce monthly film shorts based on scenes from their live show with the help of filmmaker Jonathan Evans. They can also be heard on the INO Broadcasting Network in their weekly comedy/sports podcast *Trew to the Game.*

In 2009, they co-founded The New Movement, which is an improv, sketch, and standup comedy theater with locations in Austin and New Orleans.